W9-CFK-649

Great

Grammar Lessons That Work

Using Poems, Picturebooks, Games, and Writing Activities to Teach Grammar and Help Students Become Better Writers

by Lee Karnowski

SCHOLASTIC
PROFESSIONAL BOOKS

New York • Toronto • London • Auckland • Sydney
Mexico City • New Delhi • Hong Kong

✧·ᐧ·ᐧ·▸·ᐧ·ᐧᐧ▸·ᐧ·ᐧ◆·ᐧ·ᐧ▸·ᐧᐧᐧ▸·ᐧᐧᐧ◆·ᐧᐧ·▸·ᐧᐧ◆·ᐧᐧᐧ◆·ᐧᐧᐧ·◆·ᐧᐧ·ᐧᐧ◆·ᐧᐧ·◆·ᐧᐧ·◆·ᐧᐧᐧ◆

Credits

First stanza of "A Sentence" and "Adjectives," "Verbs," "Pronouns," "Conjunctions," "Question Mark," "Exclamation Mark," and "Dash" from *Words Words Words* by Mary O'Neill. Copyright © 1966 by Mary O'Neill. Copyright renewed 1994 by Erin Baroni and Abigail Hagler. Used by permission of Marian Reiner.

"Sound of Water" from *What is That Sound!* by Mary O'Neill. Copyright © 1966 by Mary O'Neill. Copyright renewed 1994 by Erin Baroni and Abigail Hagler. Used by permission of Marian Reiner.

"What is Gray?" from *Hailstones and Hailbut Bones* by Mary O'Neill and Leonard Weisgard, III., copyright © 1961 by Mary LeDuc O'Neill. Used by permission of Doubleday, a division of Random House, Inc.

"Johnny" from *That Was Summer* by Marci Ridlon. Copyright © 1969 by Marci Ridlon and used with permission of the author.

"Woodpecker" copyright © 1990 by Jane Yolen. Appears in *Birdwatch* by Jane Yolen, published by Philomel Books, a division of Penguin Putnam Books for Young Readers. Published by permission of Curtis Brown, Ltd.

"Two Pterodactyls" copyright © 1990 by Jane Yolen. Appears in *Dinosaur Dances* by Jane Yolen, published by G.P. Putnam's Sons, a divison of Penguin Putnam Books for Young Readers. Published by permission of Curtis Brown, Ltd.

▸·ᐧ·ᐧ·ᐧ◆·ᐧ·ᐧ·ᐧᐧ◆·ᐧ·ᐧᐧᐧ◆·ᐧ·ᐧ·ᐧ◆·ᐧ·ᐧᐧᐧ◆·ᐧᐧ·ᐧᐧ◆·ᐧ·ᐧᐧᐧ◆·ᐧᐧ·ᐧ◆·ᐧᐧᐧ◆·ᐧᐧ·ᐧ◅

No part of this publication may be reproduced in whole or in part, stored in a retrieval system in any form or by any means, electronic or mechanical, photocopying, recording, or otherwise, without written permission of the publisher. For information regarding permission, write to Scholastic, Inc., 555 Broadway, New York, NY 10012.

Front cover design by Niloufar Safavieh
Interior design by Sydney Wright
Copyright © 2000 by Lee Karnowski
ISBN: 0-590-87303-2

Contents

Introduction

I have designed the activities in this book to introduce grammar to students in a way that delights and intrigues them. Math and science teachers have been moving toward a hands-on, discovery method of teaching, with great success. Language arts teachers must do the same. While the study of grammar does not require magnifying glasses, unifix cubes, or tangram pieces, it does require helping our students become actively involved in the study of language and how it works. I've found that the best way to do this is through a series of activities built around the same topic, and that's what you'll find compiled here.

I introduce each topic with a quick, engaging lesson, and then follow it with a few small-group activities that invite students to explore their vast knowledge of oral language and discover what they already know about grammar intuitively.

Once students have had a chance to think about the topic, we turn to literature for examples of how authors put their knowledge of grammar to work in their writing. Because it is much easier to notice patterns of language, word choice, and author's craft on a page that is not dense with print, I often choose picture books as models. These books abound in beautiful prose, and they engage older audiences, especially when they're listening or reading as aspiring writers.

After we've examined how writers craft their words, I ask students to try their hand at using their new knowledge of grammar in a short writing piece. Applying what they've learned to their own work is a crucial step. After all, a solid grounding in grammar enhances the way we speak and write, and students need plenty of practice making this connection. However, trying to apply a new technique to a five-page paper can be overwhelming. I've devised short writing activities that allow students to focus on the skill they've been exploring. Once they've internalized it, they will apply it to their own work naturally.

Each lesson includes ideas for a Writers' Wall that serves as a reference area for students as they explore various aspects of language. It's also a great place to share student work.

When you ask students, "What is your least favorite subject in school?" too often grammar heads the list. I believe it is the traditional approach to teaching grammar that has made this subject so daunting, and I hope that the new approach described here will help students become interested and excited about this fascinating study of our language.

PARTS OF SPEECH

> The names and functions of the main parts of speech
> should be taught not as an end in themselves but as a way to create
> a common vocabulary for talking about the language we speak.

The Behavior of Words

Student Objective

To understand that a word's part of speech can change from sentence to sentence because part of speech depends on how a word behaves in a sentence.

Background

A word in English can play different roles in a sentence. Words have various functions, or behaviors, which are described differently by two distinct models of grammar. Thus, depending on which grammar model you follow, word behavior is either *indicated by* or *based on* the place of the word in the sentence, what other words precede the word in question, and the form the word takes.

The two models of grammar—traditional and structural—define *noun* as follows:

Traditional grammar says that a noun is a person, place, thing, or idea.

Structural grammar says that:

◆ a noun can form a plural or show possession;

◆ a noun comes after an article and before a verb, or after the verb as an object of the verb;

◆ a noun often appears with an article, like *a* or *the*, a possessive, like *my* or *your*, or a demonstrative, like *this* or *these*.

This book will use the structural model of grammar.

Lesson

Location, Location, Location

Write *star* on the chalkboard. Ask students, *Is this word a noun, verb, or adjective?* A debate might ensue because it is impossible to tell what the part of speech it is until *star* is used in a sentence.

> A movie **star** is known throughout the country.
> She **stars** in the play.
> He was the **star** attraction.

Wrap-up

Choose a word that your students know and that can function as at least two parts of speech, such as *treasure* (noun, verb), *crack* (noun, verb, adjective), or *run* (noun, verb). It's all right to use a word that changes form when it changes function (thus *run* can be used as an adjective as *runny*), especially if you want to showcase a word from the students' reading. Write the word on the chalkboard and ask students to write three sentences, each of which uses a form of the word in a different way.

Extension Activities

Jabberworking

Reading the poem "Jabberwocky" from Lewis Carroll's *Through the Looking Glass* shows students that they know what part of speech a word is even when they may not know what the word means. When they read Carroll's invented words, they automatically find the structural clues that let them decide what those words are doing in each sentence.

You can use Carroll's original book, just the text of the poem, or a modern illustrated version, such as *Jabberwocky: A Book of Brillig Dioramas* by Graeme Base (Harry N. Abrams, 1996). First read "Jabberwocky" to the class as a whole, allowing students to enjoy the playful language. (If students don't have copies of the poem, write it out on the chalkboard before you

start.) Read it through again, stopping at invented words and asking, *What do you think these are? What could this mean? What does it **sound** like to you?* Then have students, working in pairs, rewrite the text, replacing invented words with known words that make sense in the sentence. Have students share their versions.

When the rewriting is finished, ask the students, still in pairs, to try to figure out what part of speech each invented word is.

Here is the first stanza of "Jabberwocky":

> 'Twas brillig, and the slithy toves
> Did gyre and gimble in the wabe:
> All mimsy were the borogoves,
> And the mome raths outgrabe.

Note: This can be used as a prewriting activity for "Jabbergabbing," below.

Bingo

Students can play this game in a small group, using the game board, or in a large group, using a transparency. In either case, begin with the game board on page 8 and write the following words on separate index cards:

rank	back	chance
ground	dead	pet
travel	light	spare
left	star	fit

Students decide where to begin. They choose a space, such as "Adjective," and then choose a word card. They must then use the word on the card as an adjective in a complete sentence in order to place a marker in the Adjective space. Then the other team has a chance to place a marker, and so on. The first team to get four in a row wins. The other team can block at any point.

Can Ties Tie?

Homographs, or words written identically but which have different meanings, illustrate that words play specific and different roles in a sentence. One resource for this activity is *What's A Frank Frank? Tasty Homograph Riddles* by Giulio Maestro (Clarion Books, 1984). Using Maestro's book and other riddles your students think of, write a riddle on the bottom of one card and the answer at the top of another card. (Each card should have a riddle answer at the top and a different riddle at the bottom; make enough cards so every student has one.) Pass out the cards and ask a student, or begin yourself, to read a riddle question. The student with the correct answer reads that answer and then reads the next question, at the bottom of the card.

Literature Connection

Most books include words that can have two meanings, depending on the roles of the words in sentences. Here are books that deliberately play with word meaning:

Eye Spy: A Mysterious Alphabet
by Linda Bourke, 1991, The Trumpet Club, NY
Illustrates homonyms for letters of the alphabet. For example, for K, keys on an organ and keys for a door are pictured. M shows a king and queen as monarchs and a butterfly as a monarch.

Amelia Bedelia Helps Out
by Peggy Parish, 1979, Avon Books, NY
(Any Amelia Bedelia book works well.)

The Accidental Zucchini: An Unexpected Alphabet
by Max Grover, 1993, Harcourt Brace & Co., Orlando
Each letter is represented by an unusual combination of objects. Nouns become adjectives.

    Apple autos
    Bathtub boat
    Cupcake canyon

What's a Frank Frank? Tasty Homograph Riddles
by Giulio Maestro, 1984, Clarion Books, NY
Students will enjoy riddles such as:

    What's a class with class?
    Students with style.

Write a Wrong

Explain to students that we can learn about the many meanings some words have by finding the words that Amelia misuses. Model how to find such words first, showing your students how placement determines meaning. Then have students compile a list of the words. This list can be recorded on the Writers' Wall. When it's compiled, have students write an Amelia Bedelia spin-off as a group.

Here are some words to begin your list:

rose	rock	fall	date
back	set	club	dive
bark	star	trip	tower
weed	chair	sink	table

One student of mine wrote:
Amelia read her job list. It said, "Amelia get some dates." She did. She got a lunch date with a friend and a movie date with her cousin.

Another page might read:
Miss Emma said, "Amelia sink the ball." So she put the ball in the sink.

Jabbergabbing

Let students write their own poem of invented words. If they like, they may even illustrate it. The original poem and drawings can then be collected as a class book.

Noun X-ing

Students can use the book *The Accidental Zucchini* as a model. They choose two nouns, then turn one of the nouns into an adjective and draw the resulting thing.

Writers' Wall

As students become aware of words that can be used in a number of positions and functions, have them write sentences that use the words and post them on the Writers' Wall.

Word Bingo

Adj.	Noun	Verb	Noun	Adj.	Noun
Verb	Adj.	Noun	Verb	Verb	Adj.
Adj.	Verb	Verb	Adj.	Noun	Adj.
Noun	Verb	Adj.	Verb	Noun	Verb
Adj.	Adj.	Noun	Verb	Adj.	Noun
Noun	Verb	Adj.	Adj.	Verb	Noun
Verb	Adj.	Noun	Verb	Noun	Adj.

Common Nouns

Student Objective

To understand the role of the common noun.

Background

Of course we all know the definition of a noun as a word that names a person, place, thing, or idea. But, again, a word's part of speech is determined by its function in a sentence, so a word that is in one situation a noun, in another can be a verb or adjective. For instance, the word *pet* is a noun when used in the sentence *I want a* **pet**. In the sentence *Please* **pet** *the dog!*, the word *pet* is a verb.

Structural grammar points out that, in the first sentence, *pet* is a noun because it is introduced by a determiner or article, and it can change its form to express singular, plural, or possessive. In the second sentence, we know *pet* is a verb because it changes form based on its subject—*[you] please pet; he pets*—and tense—*today, you pet; yesterday, you petted.*

And *pet* can also be an adjective: *My* **pet** *snake sleeps all day.* Since *pet* comes before the noun *snake*, we know it's an adjective.

Lesson

Found Nouns

Choose a poem that has quite a few nouns. Ask students to underline the nouns, discussing why they think the words are nouns. Before you read the poem to your class, you can introduce the concepts of place in a sentence and word form as determining part of speech. Marci Ridlon's poem "Johnny," from the collection *Read-Aloud Rhymes for the Very Young*, selected by Jack Prelutsky

(Knopf, 1986), is a good one to start with.

Johnny

To Johnny a box
is a house
or a car
or a ship
or a train
or a horse.
A stick
is a sword
or a spear
or a cane,
and a carpet
is magic,
of course.

Wrap-up

Discuss with students the results of their noun search. Were they successful? If so, ask them how they knew which words were the nouns. If they weren't successful, ask them what proved tricky about identifying nouns.

Extension Activities

ORAL LANGUAGE

Noun Chain

Students can find common nouns around the classroom by playing this listing game for small groups. The first player begins the game by finding or thinking of a thing and naming it. The next player must then add a new noun to the list, but that second noun must link to the first by beginning with the last letter of the first noun. For example, the first player might say, *Blackboard*. Then the second player could say, *Door*, the third, *Room*, the fourth, *Map*, and so on.

Teaching Nouns Their ABC's

Students form groups of three or four. Each group has a sheet with noun categories listed down the left side. A student volunteer chooses a letter of the alphabet for the whole class; all words compiled for each category must begin with this letter. Groups receive one point for each answer that begins with the right letter, is a common noun, and fits its category. (Three to four minutes should be long enough for this game.) A game sheet for the letter *P* might look as follows:

food items	peanuts, peaches, popcorn
occupations	postal worker, politician
school items	pencil, paper
places in a city	park
a person's feelings	peacefulness
flowers and trees	pansies, petunias
an animal	panther, porcupine

Score: 13

Dictionary

Have a student find a noun in the dictionary that the rest of the class probably doesn't know. (Remind the class what a noun is.) On the chalkboard the student writes the word's correct definition plus two other definitions which are incorrect. The student numbers the definitions 1, 2, and 3; caution them not to always put the correct definition as number 1. The object for the rest of the class is to figure out which definition is the correct one; students write down the number of the definition they choose. (This is a version of the commercial game *Balderdash*.)

For example, the chalkboard might read:

obeisance:
1. a gesture of respect
2. a command to obey
3. a gaping hole

This game can be played by the whole class or in groups of six or eight, with one student reading the chosen word and the three definitions, in any order. (The student choosing the word may, of course, make up incorrect definitions.) As above, the other players write down the number of the definition they think is correct.

When everyone has written down a number, the first player reads the word, the correct number, and the definition. Players who choose the right definition receive one point.

Literature Connection

Alphabet books are great for identifying nouns because they sort them by letter and illustrate them. Below are two alphabet books, presenting a variety of nouns, that you might want to use in your classroom.

Grandmother's Alphabet: Grandma Can Be Anything From A to Z
by Eve Shaw, 1997, Pfeifer-Hamilton Publishers, Duluth

Grandma is an Artist
She paints with colors bright.

Grandma can be...
an actress, an author, or an architect...and so can I.

The Sailor's Alphabet
illustrated by Michael McCurdy, 1998, Houghton Mifflin, Boston
This book presents chanteys of sailors of the 1800s.

Oh, A is the anchor and that you all know...

This next book presents nouns through lighthearted rhyme:

A Mink, A Fink, A Skating Rink: What Is a Noun?
by Brian P. Cleary, 1999, Carolrhoda Books, Minneapolis

Hill is a noun.
Mill is a noun.
Even Uncle Phil is a noun.

Noun Abecedaries

Students can make books for younger students. After looking at how adult authors write alphabet books, students can write their own ABC Noun Books. These can have themes, such as toys, buildings, animals, or any topic that might appeal to a young child.

It All Adds Up

Invite your students to write an addition "word problem" by choosing four or five nouns that belong together as a category. For example:

sandwiches	jackets
salads	mittens
cakes	scarf
sunshine	+ hat
+ ants	
picnic	winter

Encourage students to try writing a more difficult version of word problems by restricting their choice of noun words to four or five that start with consecutive letters of the alphabet.

apples	rocks
bananas	sand
cherries	towels
+ dates	+ undertow
fruit	beach

Writers' Wall

Invite students to add unusual nouns to the Writers' Wall that they can use to spice up their writing.

Proper Nouns

Student Objective

To determine whether a noun is proper and needs to be capitalized.

Background

The word *noun* means *name*, thus a *common noun* is the name for something common, or general (a person, place, thing, or idea), and is not capitalized. A *proper noun* is the name of something specific (it is the thing's name) and is always capitalized. This difference is straightforward enough, but a word can be used as both a common and proper noun, so deciding whether to capitalize the word can be difficult. Here are a few examples that may help:

Words that used to be considered proper nouns may no longer be capitalized because,

through long usage, they have come to be considered common nouns. The names of the seasons come under this category: summer, spring, winter, fall. Also, the cardinal directions are not capitalized (north, south, east, west), but the names of regions of the U.S. are considered proper nouns. Thus: *Drive north from New York City for 20 miles, and you'll be at the East Coast of New England.*

General academic subjects (history, math, science) are not capitalized. Specific course names, however, are proper nouns and are capitalized. Thus: *I like math because there are definite answers; Earth Science has definite answers, too, but it bores me.*

Words for relatives are proper nouns, and so capitalized, only if they come before the person's given name or substitute for that name. Thus, they are an appellation or part of one (Uncle Bob, Aunt Evelyn, Grandpa). So when referring to a specific relative, whether using the relative's given name or not, the word for the relative is capitalized (*I must ask Mother and Father if I may go to the cinema. Grandpa, can we get ice cream?*). Another way to think about it is if the word for the relative can be replaced with the person's name, then the word must be capitalized. But when referring to a relative generally, and the person's name *cannot* replace the word for the relative, then the word is a proper noun and not capitalized (*My aunt and uncle will be staying at our house. The best relatives are grandparents*).

    (Thanks to *Dr. Grammar's Writes from Wrongs* by Richard Tracz, 1991, Vintage Books, NY for these sub-rules.)

Lesson

Proper Nouns are We, Wherever We Are

Call on four or five students to provide the information for the following sentence:

I, _____, was born in the month of _____ in the city of _____ in the state of _____.
I, Janice Cummings, was born in the month of July in the city of Chicago in the state of Illinois.

    Explain to students that the capital letters indicate proper nouns. These nouns are not general nouns but specific ones—the *names* of a person, a month, a city, and a state.

Wrap-up

Challenge students to write a brief description of their families, including the names of their relatives and where they live, in which all proper nouns are properly capitalized and common nouns are not.

    Alternatively, challenge them to write stories for which they must invent at least two

characters who, for any reason students choose, must interact. Again, the idea is to be sure to capitalize proper nouns but not common nouns. And encourage students to come up with several proper nouns, reminding them that anything that is referred to by name, such as a business, a pet, even a car, is a proper noun.

Extension Activities

I Went on a Trip to...

Many children know the game "I went to the store and bought...," which requires students to add items in alphabetical order to a group list. This adaptation focuses students on proper nouns. Instead of listing items purchased, students try to alphabetically string together the names of states and cities or, even harder, states and capitals. (Of course, students can name any capital or state that begins with the right letter; it would be impossible to alphabetically string states and capitals that belonged together.) *I went on a trip to Alaska. I went on a trip to Alaska and Boise.* At each turn, the player must repeat the cities and states already mentioned and then add one more.

    Although the whole class can play at once, in smaller groups everyone can have more than one turn.

Properly Common or Commonly Proper

On the chalkboard, in a jumble, write a few general and specific place names that students are sure to know. (If you are from Minnesota, for instance, maybe write: *Minneapolis, park, The Walker Art Center, zoo, stadium.*) Also write the category titles "Proper" and "Common." Then challenge students to identify which nouns are specific and go under "Proper" and which are general and go under "Common." Then let students brainstorm other nouns for each category. Point out that some of the common nouns could be transformed to proper nouns if they were called by name (e.g., *Minnesota Zoo*).

Proper	Common
New York City	street
Central Park	block
Yankee Stadium	library
Fifth Avenue	theater

Literature Connection

The first two books below showcase names and other proper nouns:

Chrysanthemum
by Kevin Henkes, 1991, The Trumpet Club, NY

> "It's so long," said Jo.
> "It scarcely fits on your name tag," said Rita, pointing.
> "I'm named after my grandmother," said Victoria.

Swamp Angel
by Anne Isaacs, 1994, The Trumpet Club, NY

> Swamp Angel decided to keep Thundering Tarnation's pelt as a rug. It was too big for Tennessee, so she moved to Montana and spread that bear rug out on the ground in front of her cabin.

These books showcase place names:

Postcards From Pluto
by Loreen Leedy, 1993, Scholastic Inc., NY
Each postcard is addressed to its recipient.

> Luna Cee
> 100 Crescent Ave.
> Crater Lake, OR
> U.S.A. 97604

The Alphabet Atlas
by Arthur Yorinks, 1999, Winslow Press, Delray Beach, FL

> A Australia is the flattest country in the world and the only nation that is also a continent.
> B Brazil is home to the world's largest tropical rainforest.

The Armadillo From Amarillo
by Lynne Cherry, 1994, The Trumpet Club, NY

> They flew so high up into the sky
> that Texas they saw below—
> the part they call the Panhandle—
> and the state of New Mexico.

The next book contains wonderful proper nouns, though the flower names are capitalized incorrectly (the good thing about the error is that it's helpful for kids, and they love to see adults' mistakes):

Allison's Zinnia
by Anita Lobel, 1990, A Mulberry Paperback Book, NY

> Maryssa misted a Magnolia for Nancy.
> Nancy noticed a Narcissus for Olga.
> Olga ordered an Orchid for Paulette.

This last book abounds in proper and common nouns:

A My Name Is Alice
by Jane Bayer, 1984, Dial Books for Young Readers, NY

> L my name is Lucy and my husband's name is Luke. We come from London and we sell leaves. Lucy is a LEMMING. Luke is a LOON.

> M my name is Maude and my husband's name is Martin. We come from Manchester and we sell mops. Maude is a MOOSE. Martin is a MOLE.

City, Village, Hamlet, Burg

In small groups, students write "city chants." Ask them to find interesting city names on a map of their state, then write the names on strips of paper. When the group has collected 25-35 names, they arrange the pieces of paper with the names on them until they have an order that creates a chant they like. (Students may think of this as old-fashioned word processing.) They do not need to use all the city names they find. One group member copies the chant on a fresh sheet of paper, and then the group practices their chant until they can present it to the class.

Wisconsin
Dairyland,
Land O Lakes, Shell Lake, Fox Lake,
Balsam Lake, Clear Lake, Moose Lake,
  Cable,
Hillsboro, Bear Creek, Pittsville,
  Perkinstown,
Hamburg, Norwalk, Sheboygan,
  Mansfield,
Parrish, Cumberland, Lakewood,
Sturgeon Bay, Green Bay, Menominee,
  Eureka!

You can publish the chants by attaching

them to a posterboard shape of your state.

Even Old New York was Once New Amsterdam

While searching their state map for names of cities, students can also keep track of interesting names of lakes and rivers. They can then write an imaginative paragraph about how the river or lake received its name.

Writers' Wall

Post amusing, exotic, and confounding names of people and places on the Writers' Wall.

Plural and Collective Nouns

Student Objective

To understand that nouns can be plural and collective.

Background

Many nouns take irregular forms in the plural, which can make them difficult to learn. This section offers activities that let students become familiar with a variety of irregular plural nouns.

Lesson

Mouse, Mice: House, Hice?

The poem below demonstrates for students that there are many exceptions to the "add s" rule for making plurals—so many, in fact, that it really isn't correct to call it a rule. Read the poem aloud to the class and invite them, singly or

together, to try to form the correct plurals before they hear you read them. This lesson is also a chance to discuss collective nouns. Ask them first, for instance, *What do we call a collection of birds?* Then ask them, *What would you call a collection of boxes?*

We'll begin with a box, and the plural is boxes;
But the plural of ox is oxen, not oxes.
One fowl is goose, but two are called geese,
Yet the plural of mouse is never meese.
You may find a lone mouse, or a whole lot of mice,
But the plural of house is houses, not hice.
If the plural of man is always called men,
Why shouldn't the plural of pan be called pen?
The cow in the plural may be called cows or kine,
But the plural of vow is vows, not vine.
And I speak of a foot, and you show me your feet,
But I give you a boot—would a pair be called beet?
If one is a tooth, and a whole set are teeth,
Why shouldn't the plural of booth be called beeth?
If the singular is this, and the plural is these,
Should the plural of kiss be nicknamed kese?
Then one may be that, and three may be those,

Yet the plural of hat would never be hose.
We speak of a brother, and also of brethren,
But though we say mother, we never say methren.
The masculine pronouns are he, his, and him,
But imagine the feminine she, shis, and shim!
So our English, I think you all will agree,
Is the trickiest language you ever did see.

—Anonymous

Wrap-up

Challenge students to write their own lists of singular and plural nouns in two columns, one headed "Singular," the other "Plural." Let them repeat some of the nouns in the poem (this may be a hard activity for some students, and they'll already have the poem in their heads), but encourage them to think up different nouns, too.

Extension Activities

Trading Forms

Pair students and challenge them to write a four-line story, one of the pair writing in the singular and the other writing in the plural. The paired students then trade stories and try, while reading aloud, to change the partner's story from the form it's in (singular or plural) to the other form. Students will quickly realize that there are more changes to be made than just the forms of the nouns.

Collective Bargaining

Read aloud from *A Cache of Jewels and Other Collective Nouns* by Ruth Heller (cited below). Then give each group of four or five students a bag containing more than one of the same item, such as hundreds of paper clips; many pencils; broken, whole, white, and colored pieces of chalk; and so on. Challenge students to think together of an appropriate name for their collection of items. Help them by

pointing out that many names for collections of things suit that collection—for instance, we say a *plague* of locust or a *brood* of hens. Have students write their idea on a separate paper and pass the bag to the next group. When everyone has had a chance to invent a collective noun for each of the bags, share the ideas. You may want to include these collective nouns for common items on the Writers' Wall.

Literature Connection

The first two books are compendiums of collective nouns:

A Cache of Jewels and Other Collective Nouns
by Ruth Heller, 1987, Grosset & Dunlap, NY

> a BOUQUET of flowers
> a SWARM of bees
> a KINDLE of kittens
> a POD of peas

A Rattle of Bones: A Halloween Book of Collective Nouns
by Kipling West, 1999, Orchard Books, NY

> a VENOM of spiders
> a WAKE of vultures
> an UNKINDNESS of ravens
> a PARLIAMENT of owls

The next book presents specific and unusual names for baby animals:

A Pinky is a Baby Mouse and Other Baby Animal Names
by Pam Munoz Ryan, 1997, Hyperion Paperbacks for Children, NY

> Baby pigs are piglets
> wallowing in a pen.
> Kids are baby goats
> ramming now and then.
> Baby pigeons are squabs
> perched near the windowpane.
> I am a baby mouse.
> Tell me, what's my name?

The final book presents the variety of ways English nouns can alter form (or not!) in the plural:

Your Foot's on My Feet: and Other Tricky Nouns by Mervin Terban, 1986, Clarion Books, NY

Collected Nouns or Perplexing Plurals

After students have added collective nouns from their reading and from "Collective Bargaining" (above) to the Writers' Wall, let them write their own books about collective nouns. They might want to use a format similar to that of *A Cache of Jewels and Other Collective Nouns*. Or, like the anonymous piece above, they could write poems (theirs may certainly be free verse) that explore the difficulties of writing plurals.

Plural Handbooks

Challenge students separately or in small groups to write their own "Handbook for Spelling Plurals." They can collect tricky nouns from their reading (*Your Foot's on My Feet: and Other Tricky Nouns* is a

great place to start). One procedure you might suggest to your students is to write the singular and plural of a chosen noun at the top of each page, then on that page write two sentences, one for each form of the word. When the text is written, students may illustrate the page. When all the students have finished writing their texts, they can order the pages alphabetically and create a classroom copy (which might be useful for editing sessions).

Writers' Wall

Students can add the collective nouns they invented during Collective Bargaining as well as interesting plural nouns found in their readings. You may want to divide space into regular plurals (those that end with /s/, /es/, /ies/ and /ves/) and irregular plurals. (Ruth Heller's *Merry-Go-Round* [Grosset & Dunlap, 1990] is another good source for plural nouns.)

◆·•·•·•·◇·•·•·•·•·◇·•·•·•·•·◇·•·•·•·◇·•·•·•·•·◇·•·•·•·•·◇

Abstract Nouns

Student Objective

To identify and understand abstract nouns.

Background

Abstract nouns, which name ideas, emotions, and feelings rather than concrete things, are confusing for many students. Before teaching this lesson and the accompanying activities, compile a list of abstract nouns to write on the chalkboard for this lesson.

Lesson

You Can't See or Touch Them, But They're Things

Concrete nouns are easy to handle because they name physical things that kids know from experience or can imagine without much strain. But abstract nouns name intangibles and so may confound students. Abstract nouns include *noun, information, quarrel, happiness, democracy, fear, loneliness, anger, friendship, beauty, bravery, love, sadness,* and *hatred,* to name a few.

Students can brainstorm other abstract nouns and post them on the Writers' Wall. Have a dictionary at hand to help students understand which form of the word is a noun— for example, *beauty* is a noun, but *beautiful* is not; *loneliness* is a noun, but *lonely* is not.

Wrap-up

Ask students to write their own definitions of abstract. When they have completed them, ask for volunteers to share their definitions with the class, and then as a class discuss the results. Ask, *What do you find the clearest way to think about what abstract means? Which definition makes the most sense to you?* If there is consensus about the best definition, post it on the Writers' Wall.

It may be better to leave the individual defining of *concrete* for another day, so that the two ideas do not become confused.

Extension Activities

I Can't See It, But I Know What It Is

Divide students into groups of four to six. Groups pick an abstract noun from the Writers' Wall and then take turns brainstorming details that bring the abstract noun to life. For example:

Fear is:
◆ creaking in the middle of the night
◆ meeting a roomful of strangers
◆ trying something dangerous that you do not know you can do, like parachuting
◆ making a speech to your peers
(Note: This is a useful prewriting activity for "A Free Verse Handle.")

I Can't See It, But I Know What It Would Say

Have student pairs choose two abstract nouns as characters and write a conversation for them.

"I am love, and I feel we should be kind to everyone."
"I am hatred, and I feel we should be susipicious of everyone."
"I make the world a peaceful place."
"I make the world dangerous and exciting!"

Literature Connection

Use abstract nouns as themes for grouping picture books. Invite students to identify which theme category on the Writers' Wall books belong in. Then let them write the title of the book and the author under the category title. For example:

Bravery

Brave Irene by William Steig, 1986, Farrar, Straus & Giroux, NY

Swamp Angel by Anne Isaacs, 1994, The Trumpet Club, NY

Nessa's Fish by Nancy Luenn, 1990, Atheneum, NY

Once When I Was Scared by Helena Clare Pittman, 1988, Puffin Unicorn Books, NY

Curiosity

Armadillo Rodeo by Jan Brett, 1995, Scholastic Inc., NY

The Story About Ping by Margorie Flack, 1933, Puffin Books, NY

Some Smug Slug by Pamela Duncan Edwards, 1996, HarperCollins Publishers, NY

Perseverance and Patience

Mike Mulligan and His Steam Shovel by Virginia Burton, 1939, Houghton Mifflin, Boston

Tikki Tikki Tembo by Arlene Mosel, 1968, Holt, Rinehart and Winston, NY

A Free Verse Handle

Have students write a free verse poem for which they must use abstract nouns they brainstormed during "You Can't See or Touch Them…" If they've also already described abstract nouns for "I Can't See It, but I Know What It Is," they may include their descriptions in their poems. If they have not yet described abstract nouns, let them begin this activity by writing five to eight descriptive phrases on separate strips of paper that they can then arrange in any order or throw away, depending on what they want finally to include in their poems. (Writing phrases on strips is also a great way to brainstorm.) When the poems are complete, publish them on a poster or in a class book.

Diamantes

Students can write a *diamante poem* using pairs of opposite abstract nouns:

fear/bravery   loneliness/comfort
love/hatred   happiness/sadness
democracy/tyranny

This type of poetry usually shifts from one meaning to its opposite at a middle point where two opposite nouns meet. Here the shift occurs at line four. The poem follows this pattern (for this lesson, the nouns should be abstract):

Noun
Adjective, adjective
Verb, verb, verb
Noun, noun/noun, noun
Verb, verb, verb
Adjective, adjective
Noun

Sadness
Downcast, unhappy
Moping, crying, sleeping,
Hurt, pain, cheerfulness, pleasure
Agreeing, cheering, loving
Contented, ecstatic
Happiness

This activity is easier and more exciting if students can use a thesaurus.

Writers' Wall

List abstract nouns gathered during "You Can't See or Touch Them, but They're Things." These words can be used as themes for categorizing picture books. (See above.)

◆·᛫·᛫·᛫·◆·᛫·᛫·◆·᛫·᛫·᛫·◆·᛫·᛫·◆·᛫··᛫·◆·᛫··᛫·◆·᛫··◆

Adjectives

Student Objective

To understand that an adjective is a word that provides additional information about a noun.

Background

The structural definition of an adjective tells us that these words often occur before the nouns they modify or after a linking verb. Adjectives can change form, becoming comparative or superlative, by adding *-er* or *-est* to the end of them or by adding *more* or *most* before them. Most students adore adjectives and tack them on abundantly to every noun. Our task as teachers is to help students use adjectives purposefully, to enhance meaning, not obscure it.

Present students with examples of adjectives coming before nouns, as well as predicate adjectives, which sneak up on a reader after a linking verb:

The *brave* hunter stalked the bear.
The hunter, who stalked the bear, was *brave*.

Lesson

Adjectives Are the Clothes Nouns Wear

Explain the role of adjectives to your students, illustrating their behavior in sentences on the chalkboard. Discuss the importance in writing of choosing adjectives for their accurate describing of nouns. Then choose your own adjective, and ask students to spend two minutes thinking of nouns that could be accurately described by it. You might write the adjective on the chalkboard and, after the two minutes, call on students for their matching nouns.

Huge
elephant
skyscraper
hippopotamus
appetite

When students have the hang of the exercise, let each one choose an adjective, write it at the head of a page, and then think up nouns it accurately modifies. But be aware: many, if not all, of your students will naturally realize that adjectives can exaggerate or contradict for ironic or comic effect, and it's great that they figure this out. Still, you may want them to focus on accurate adjectives now, so that you know they understand the difference; or you may think it fine that they mix it up. That, of course, is up to you.

Wrap-up

Ask students to write their names in the center of a page and list under it three to five adjectives they think accurately describe them. Then have them write *lion*, *chicken*, *building*, and *Martian*, each at a corner of the page. Under each new word (all nouns by the way), they then write three to five adjectives that they think the creature named, if it were looking at them, would use to describe them. From this play, students learn that the accuracy of adjectives depends on point of view, and that accuracy itself is relative.

Extension Activities

Smaller Than a Bread Box?

Give each student a paper bag for holding an object they choose from home or school. On the outside of the bags, they write their names and four adjectives describing the object inside, then staple the bags closed. Students present their adjectives to the class and call on classmates to guess the identity of the object. They may come up with additional adjectives if the class needs extra clues. This activity will help students choose useful, specific adjectives.

Adjective Addition

Collect pairs of leaves, buttons, fabric squares, or canceled stamps. Give each student an envelope containing one item of a pair, making sure that another student has the matching item. Students look inside their envelopes (not removing the items) and write on the envelope four adjectives that describe the item. Students now try to find the match to their items according to the adjectives written on the envelopes. When all the items are paired, discuss with students the kinds of adjectives they found helpful and unhelpful.

orange	orange-red
triangular	two-holed
small	triangular
+ two-holed	+ plastic
button	button

These two buttons are probably a match.

Literature Connection

Examine the adjectives in any book the class is reading. Ask, *Which adjectives give you a clear mental picture of the character?* (or scene or villain, and so on). And, *Do any of the adjectives sound like what they mean? Would you have used a different word? Why?*

Below are some picture books that concentrate on adjectives. They were written for younger children but use adjectives effectively.

A is for Angry: An Animal and Adjective Alphabet by Sandra Boynton, (Workman Publishing, 1983)
Animals in the illustrations show the emotion named.

> A is for ANGRY
> B is for BASHFUL
> C is for CLEAN
> D is for DIRTY.

A Children's Zoo
by Tana Hoban, 1981, Mulberry Books, NY
For each animal, Hoban gives three clues: two adjectives and one verb. (This is a useful model for easy riddles.)

> black
> white
> waddles
> PENGUIN

Lunch
by Denise Fleming, 1996, Henry Holt and Company, NY

> Mouse was very hungry. He was so hungry, he ate a crisp white–turnip,
> tasty orange–

The next book lightheartedly presents adjectives:

On the Go: A Book of Adjectives
by B. Maestro & G. Maestro, 1988, Crown Books for Young Readers, NY.

Picturing Adjectives

Invite students to illustrate the meaning of an adjective of their choice by drawing the word in such a way that it *looks like* its definition. Publish the results in a "Picture This Adjective" book.

Concrete Poems = Visual Adjectives

Students choose a theme, such as spring, Halloween, animals, and so on, and then decide on an object or character that represents the theme. Next, they think of at least 20 adjectives that describe that object or character, relating it, of course, to the theme. (They'll need plenty of adjectives for the next step.) Students then sketch the object or character and fill up the sketch with adjectives or outline it with adjectives. Those who like a challenge can try to create the shape of the object or character with just the words, without sketching it first. When the poems are finished, remind students to write their themes as titles at the top of the page. These, too, can be collected into a great class book.

A good book of concrete poetry is *Doodle Dandies: Poems That Take Shape* by J. Patrick Lewis (Atheneum Books for Young Readers, 1998).

Strings of Shiny, Silky, Precious...

Have students write string poems of adjectives in order to describe people who are important to them. For example:

> Funny,
> Sensitive,
> Loving,
> Understanding,
> Supportive,
> Kind,
> My grandma, Betty.

Writers' Wall

Post super adjectives that students collect from their reading. Of course, you might want to compile your own list, too, to start them off or make sure certain adjectives appear on the wall.

Precise Adjectives

Student Objective

To understand that adjectives must be precise to be useful to the reader.

Background

Too many adjectives blur meaning and diminish the impact of our writing. On the other hand, the right adjective can startle, coax, or amuse the reader. The writer must choose adjectives carefully if the writing is to be powerful.

This section offers ways to reinforce the value of precise adjectives through reading and discussion of literature.

Lesson

Adjective Sharpening

Have students sit in a circle. Talk with the class about the role of adjectives and why precise adjectives are important. Then take out a small toy and describe the toy or some aspect of it. If the object is a small squirrel plush toy, for instance, you might say, a *bushy tail*, and pass it to another student. That student must then describe the toy differently, perhaps saying, *tan fur*, and passing it to the next student. Continue around the circle until descriptives have been exhausted; this may happen before the circuit is complete. Then begin the activity again with another object.

Wrap-up

Discuss the lesson with the class. Ask, *Which*

adjectives do you remember being especially successful? Why do you think they were effective? You may have to delicately point out some of the ineffective choices. Ask, *Why do you think* big (for example) *wasn't a strong choice?* Lead the class to discover that general adjectives, such as *big*, *small*, or *nice*, don't convey much of importance about what they set out to describe.

Extension Activities

Word Paint

Go to a paint store and pick out color sample strips for your class. Each strip should include many shades of the same general color; cut the strips into chips. In small groups students must come up with an adjective that *precisely* describes each shade, writing their choices on separate scraps of paper. Number each description, and write the corresponding number on the back of the paint chip each adjective describes. Then the groups mix up their paint chips, pass them to another group, and that group then tries to match the adjectives to the paint chips they describe. If they are successful, the original group did a great job of describing their variety of color shades.

Please Be Precise

As a class, brainstorm adjectives for precisely describing a variety of nouns. Then go back and cross out any that are vague or redundant and add new, provocative ones. Explain to the class that this is exactly what authors do when they revise their writing in order to improve it before it's published.

baby

~~small~~	smelly	~~tiny~~	wet
crabby	soft	colicky	~~young~~

The Never-Closed-to-Adjectives Cloze

Challenge student pairs to write a sentence that includes three nouns, leaving a space before each noun for an adjective. Students then number the blank spaces and, on a separate sheet, list the adjectives they would choose for the blank spaces. They then pass the sentence to the next group, which records their choices of adjectives on their own sheet of lists, and so on. When all groups have had a chance to complete every sentence, share the results.

The 1. _____ lady walked along the 2. _____ street followed by her 3. _____ cat.

Original Group	Second Group
1. cranky	1. old
2. city	2. dark
3. ancient	3. curious

Literature Connection

Here are three books to share which revel in precise adjectives:

Toad
by Ruth Brown, 1996, Dutton Children's Books, NY

A muddy toad, a mucky toad,
a clammy, sticky, gooey toad,
odorous, oozing, foul and filthy,
and dripping with venomous fluid.

North Country Night
by Daniel San Souci, 1990, A Picture Yearling Book, NY

Under the winter moon the great horned owl glides over the roof of the cabin and circles above the tops of the giant pine trees. He is searching for prey with his keen yellow eyes.

Many Luscious Lollipops
by Ruth Heller, 1989, Grosset & Dunlap, NY
An ADJECTIVE's terrific
When you want to be specific.
It easily identifies

By number, color or by size.
TWELVE LARGE,
BLUE, GORGEOUS
Butterflies.

The next book delights in evocative adjectives:

All the Colors of the Earth
by Sheila Hamanaka, 1994, Mulberry Paperback Books, NY

Children come in all colors of the earth—
The roaring browns of bears and soaring eagles,
The whispering golds of late summer grasses,
And crackling russets of fallen leaves…

We Were Introduced by the Most Wonderful Adjective

Have students choose a character from their reading and write a character sketch. Explain to them that a character sketch describes not only what the character looks like, but how the character behaves and thinks. Encourage students to use unusual but precise adjectives that make us pause and say to ourselves, *I know just what the author of the sketch was thinking about this character. It's like meeting the character!*

Adjectives Advertise

Ask students to write advertisements for products. Explain to them that professional ad-writers look for just the right adjectives to make products seem appealing so that people will want to buy them.

"Buy Crunchy Munchy Cereal because it stays crunchy in the bowl, and the munchy taste of fresh strawberries will wake up your sleepy tastebuds."

Writers' Wall

Keep track of wonderful adjectives that students find in their reading. Encourage them to replace tired adjectives in their writing with the ones posted on the Wall.

Comparative and Superlative Adjectives

Student Objective

To understand the function of the three basic kinds of adjectives.

Background

Most students have gleaned ideas about comparison adjectives unconsciously, but it is necessary to teach the concept explicitly. Adjectives come in three kinds: *positive*, which modify nouns without comparison; and *comparative* and *superlative*, which modify nouns in relation to other nouns—*comparative* adjectives referring to one of two nouns, *superlative* adjectives referring to one of three or more nouns. This may sound difficult, but examples will clear it up:

1) The tree is *tall*.
   Tall is a positive adjective.
2) This tree is *taller* than that one.
   Taller is a comparative adjective.
3) That tree is the *tallest* one.
   Tallest is a superlative adjective.

It is also important to teach irregular adjectives, some of which are:

good, better, best
bad, worse, worst
many, more, most

Lesson

Beautifuller Than a Summer Day?

Copy the poem "Adjectives" by Mary O'Neill and use it to discuss the three basic kinds of adjective. During the discussion, try to elicit from students the fact that certain adjectives don't have simple comparative and superlative forms, but instead must be preceded by *more*, *less*, and *most*.

Adjectives

Adjectives tell you the quality of a person, place,
   or thing
As *pretty* girl, *big* city, *fast* horse, *golden* ring.
Some adjectives increase their strength
By going on to greater length:
As *pretty* when you're *positive*
she's fair,
But *prettier* whenever you *compare*,
And see a second more exquisite face
Among the members of the human race.
But *prettiest* is where you reach
the top—
Superlative—and there you have
to stop.

Wrap-up

Rather than start out with a sentence-writing drill requiring students to use comparatives and superlatives, tell students that their task is to create comparative and superlative *nouns* and *verbs*. This should yield some ridiculous words (i.e. *deskiest*, *climbier*), the effect of which, in turn, will be a fun lesson, and the activity will also unobtrusively drive home the fact that only adjectives are comparative or superlative. Of course, writing accurate comparatives and superlatives is also a valuable activity, and a straight exercise might be the perfect way to bring the class back to focus.

(Note: While working with the class on proper comparatives and superlatives, make a quiet point of correcting students' use of *then* for *than*.)

Extension Activities

Alliterative Superlative Adjective

ORAL LANGUAGE

In groups of three (or two or four, if necessary), students choose a noun together and then separately find superlative adjectives that start with the same letter as the noun.

cave: coldest, clammiest, creepiest
bat: biggest, blackest, buggiest

Dictionaries will make this activity more productive and enjoyable.

He Was Bigger Than a Small Car!

ORAL LANGUAGE

Ask students to get into groups of three (or group them yourself), explaining that each group will tell a "fish tale." The group chooses a noun as a character. The first student tells something about the noun and describes it with a positive adjective. The second student then uses the comparative form of the adjective, and the third student tells the biggest whopper of them all, using the adjective's superlative form. Hold enough rounds of "fish tales" that everyone has a chance to use the superlative form.

Here's a simple example:
The wrestler was very strong.
The wrestler was stronger than an ox.
The wrestler was the strongest athlete at the Olympics.

Literature Connection

LITERATURE CONNECTION

Tall tales are known for exaggerations of size, strength, bravery, and so on, and there are many such tales to share with students. After reading a tall tale with your students, challenge them to make comparative and superlative statements about the characters.
Two famous tall tales are:

Pecos Bill
by Steven Kellogg, 1986, William Morrow & Company, Inc., NY

> When Bill dodged the snake's fangs, it slapped its coils around him.
> The snake squeezed hard, but Bill squeezed harder and he didn't let up until every drop of poison was out of that reptile, leaving it skinny as a rope and mild as a goldfish.

The Bunyans
by Audrey Wood, 1996, The Blue Sky Press, NY

> After all that sculpting, Little Jean's shoes were full of sand. Pa knew Ma Bunyan wouldn't want her clean floors dirtied up, so he told Little Jean to sit down and empty out his shoes.
>
> The sand from Little Jean's shoes blew away on the eastern wind and settled down a state away. It covered a valley ten miles long, making sand dunes eight hundred feet high. Everyone knows that's how the Great Dunes of Colorado came to be.

The next book uses ingenious and imaginative superlatives to describe how a mother loves her two sons:

I Love You the Purplest
by Barbara M. Joosse, 1996, Chronicle Books, San Francisco, CA

> "Mama, who has the most worms?" he asked.
> Mama smiled.
> "Max, your can is full of the liveliest worms. And Julian, your can has the juiciest."

Spinning the Wildest Yarn

WRITING CONNECTION

Have students write a tall tale. They may certainly follow the format of the books mentioned above. Or perhaps your part of the country includes a famous desert, lake, or mountain that needs a tall tale to explain its existence and spread its fame. Remind students that part of their task is to use precise, ingenious comparative and superlative adjectives.

A Superlative Poem

Students can also write poems that build their form from the three basic kinds of adjective.

Little,
The dog is little.
Littler,

The puppy is littler.
Littlest,
The flea is littlest.

Writers' Wall

Students can add to the Wall all three forms of an adjective when they come across one they like. You'll probably want to post all irregular forms for easy reference.

Verbs

Student Objective

To understand the role of the action verb.

Background

Verbs are like a train's engine because they do the heavy work in a sentence: They glide or lug or speed the action that the nouns are performing, or are having performed on them. In fact, verbs are so important to writers that e. e. cummings described his, and every poet's, characteristic trait as the "ineluctable preoccupation with The Verb…"

A discussion of verbs tends to become complicated quickly (a look at Ruth Heller's *Kites Sail High* [Grosset & Dunlap, 1988] should confirm this). The traditional way to begin the study of verbs with your students is to teach them that a verb is a "doing word," or a word that means an action. Picking out the action words in a sentence may seem easy, but many students have trouble doing it and will appreciate an illustrative lesson, as well as your patience. Or try having students "test" words to see if they're

verbs, using the structural definition of verbs. For each word they think is a verb, have them use it in a few test sentences to see if it changes form: *I eat; He eats*. If the form changes, the word is a verb. Another test is to use the word in the past and present and see if it changes: *Today I eat; Yesterday I ate*. Since the form changes, we know it's a verb.

Lesson

Vital Verbs

Copy "Verbs" by Mary O'Neill (below) on the chalkboard and select a student or two to read it aloud. Ask, *What does it mean that a verb "puts [other words] into action"?* Ask the class to think up examples of "action words," and write several of their suggestions on the chalkboard around the poem. Then ask individual students to come up to the front and each act out one of the verbs. Say, for instance, *Will you show us your impression of sauntering?*

jump
roll
saunter

To words a verb's
The main attraction—
Because it puts them
Into action.

walk
jog
somersault

Wrap-up

In advance, pick a few different actions, such as walking, eating, and touching, as categories of kinds of action. Then come up with two or three other actions that fall under those categories. List the categories on the chalkboard and discuss the different denotations and connotations with your class. Ask, *Why would I write* saunter *instead of* walk? *What kind of* walking *is* sauntering, *and what does that action suggest about the person doing the action?*

You may then want to have students come up with their own categories of actions.

Walk	**Eat**	**Touch**
saunter	chomp	push
stroll	devour	stroke
meander	nibble	hit

Extension Activities

ORAL LANGUAGE

I Like to Dribble, Slide, Read, Canter, Dive, Speed...

Students can pair up according to hobbies or sports they enjoy and then try to list all of the verbs associated with their hobby or sport. For example, *biking* might include *pedaling, steering, braking, balancing,* and *coasting.*

(Note: This is a useful prewriting activity for "Concrete Story," below.)

ORAL LANGUAGE

Busy Words

Read *Sit Still* by Nancy Carlson (Puffin Books, 1996) and have small groups of students find verbs for the 101 ways Patrick knows to sit on chairs (*lounge, fall, jiggle, crawl, slouch, sprawl,* and so on). Next, students can think of 101 ways to keep Patrick busy so he doesn't have time to sit on chairs. He might *jog, play, paint, climb,* and so on. A thesaurus will help generate words.

(Note: This is a useful prewriting activity

for "Strings of Jumping, Spilling...," below.)

LITERATURE CONNECTION

Literature Connection

The first three books present vivid, exciting verbs:

Night of the Gargoyles
by Eve Bunting, 1994, The Trumpet Club, NY
> Then down they swoop
> to where a fountain splashes dark,
> the water spitting from a cherub's mouth.
> They gargoyle-hunch around the rim
> and gargoyle-grunt
> with friends from other corners
> who have come for company.

Night Noises
by Mem Fox, 1989, The Trumpet Club, NY
> Butch Aggie dozed at her feet. Outside, clouds raced along the sky, playing hide-and-seek with the moon. Wind and rain rattled at the windows, and trees banged against the roof.

North Country Night
by Daniel San Souci, 1990, A Picture Yearling Book, NY
> Soon the owl locates movement in the cool shadows below the trees. A gray coyote lopes effortlessly through the fresh snow. Although the owl is a fierce predator, he will not disturb the coyote.

The next two selections are ABC books that feature verbs:

Allison's Zinnia
by Anita Lobel, 1990, A Mulberry Paperback Book, NY
> Irene inked an Iris for Jane.
> Jane jarred a Jack-in-the-pulpit for Kathleen.
> Kathleen kept a Kalmia for Leslie.

Action Alphabet
by Shelley Rotner, 1996, Atheneum Books for Young Readers, NY
Photographs show children *arching, blowing, climbing, diving...*

Concrete Story

WRITING CONNECTION

Students can use their list of sport or hobby words brainstormed for "I Like to Dribble, Slide, Read, Canter, Dive, Speed…" to map out a story plot. Challenge them to arrange the verbs in sequence and as a physical representation of the action. So if the sport were, again, *biking*, before the story was written the page might look like this (read from the bottom, up the hill):

> braking
> coasting
> balancing
> steering
> pedaling

Inform students that they can use any form of a verb that suits the story. So the final page might look like this (start reading from the bottom):

> It was a tremendous hill, and after the hard climb braking didn't even cross my mind.
>
> At the top of the hill I took in the the view and then coasted a the way down.
>
> I had to steer around ruts and small bushes and struggled to balance because I hit rocks and roots and branches.
>
> I was pedaling my mountain bike up a steep hill.

Strings of Jumping, Spilling, Laughing, Sprawling…

WRITING CONNECTION

With the verbs they thought up for "Busy Words," students can write a string poem. If they write the verbs on cards or strips, students can move them around until they arrive at a final draft and then copy it out on a fresh page.

How to Sit on a Chair

Lounge on it,
sprawl on it,
crawl on it,
slouch on it,
droop on it,
sag on it,
jump on it,
break it!

Writers' Wall

WRITERS' WALL

Post the verbs that students brainstormed, and by all means let them add terrific verbs they find in their reading. Now they'll have a verb reference for in-class writing.

Precise Verbs

Student Objective

To use verbs precisely and learn how to substitute vivid verbs for overworked ones.

Background

If verbs are chosen for precision and vividness (i.e., strong), they will grab the reader's attention. If the verbs are weak—and common verbs get wrung out through overuse—readers will lose interest in the writing. Of course, not every verb needs to startle the reader. Choosing verbs is a question of balance between the common and the unusual, but in all cases the writer's aim is to be precise.

Lesson

She Did What? How Specific!

Discuss with the class the value of precise verbs, reminding them, if you've used it, of the "Vital Verbs" lesson. Then let volunteers read the sentences below (already written on the chalkboard). Challenge students to think of precise, evocative verbs to replace *walk*.

> He walked quietly by the bedroom door so he wouldn't wake the baby. (e.g., *tiptoed*)
> He walked quickly to the ringing phone so his sister wouldn't answer it. (*jogged*)
> She walked in step with the band in the parade. (*marched*)
> She walked slowly, looking in all the shop windows. (*strolled*)

Wrap-up

Let students share their results. Ask, for instance, *Tell me about the person who's racing to the phone* (or *hopping with the band*, and so on). *What kind of person do you picture when you read this sentence?* Lead students to articulate that the precise verbs are what bring the subject (the character) to life: The verbs relate the manner of the action and so the manner of the subject.

Extension Activities

Basketverb

Organize students into teams of five or six. Project a transparency of or post a picture that displays *action*. The teams must write as many verbs as they can think of to describe the action. Encourage students to choose precise verbs. After an allotted amount of time, ask each team for one of the verbs they came up with. Write these verbs on the chalkboard, asking if other teams also came up with that verb; those that did must cross it off their lists. Continue posting new verbs. First-announced verbs that accurately describe the action, and that other teams *have* thought of, count as two-point shots; verbs that no other team has thought of are three-pointers. At the end of the game, the team with the most points wins.

Verb Charades

Students compile sentences that have verbs which can be acted out. They write their sentences on slips of paper; the slips go into a container. Students take turns choosing a slip and acting out the sentence. The

◆·········◆···◆···◆·····◆·····◆······◆·····◆·····◆·····◆·····◆·····◆·········◆

audience calls out ideas of the action being dramatized. If no one hits on the right verb in a short time, the student reads the sentence aloud. "Verb Charades" can also be played in teams, with team members trying to figure out their performer's charade. Teams win points for guessing the correct verb. Also, the game can be made harder if the guessers are required to solve the entire sentence.

Examples of charades sentences are:

Amos *skids* to a stop.
Elizabeth *whispers* the answer.
Byron *leaps* to his feet.
Superman *soars* off the building.

Literature Connection

The previous literature connection books on verbs are also suitable for *this* lesson. *Dinosaur Dances* by Jane Yolen (G.P. Putnam's Sons, 1990) is a book of verb-rich poems students may also enjoy. Groups of students could hunt poems for vivid, precise verbs.

Two Pterodactyls

Two pterodactyls
Dancing in the moonlight,
Sliding through the night sky,
Slipping through the stars.

What's All This Flap About Verbs?

Invite students to write riddle flap books, which on the cover hint at people, animals, or objects pictured under the flap. The riddles consist of verbs that describe how the noun found inside usually behaves. Riddles might be related to a topic of study. Exhibit flap books in the class or in the hall; for an activity, group students into riddle teams.

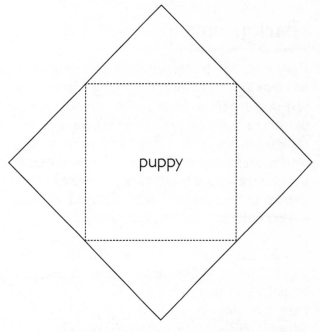

Writers' Wall

List overworked verbs and also precise verbs students can substitute for them. For example, post:

Overworked	Fresh
said	yelled
	whispered
	replied
	called
	responded
	answered

Verb Tense and Agreement

Student Objective

To understand the past, present, and future tenses.

Background

Of course, verb tenses can distinguish subtle relations of time (we often use the *present perfect*, *past perfect*, *future perfect* without even thinking about how to form them), but this section focuses on the three basic tenses, *past*, *present*, and *future*. Mastery of the basic tenses is important for your students so that they can step up to the next level as skillful readers and writers of interesting, engaging stories and reports.

Although most verbs in English form their past tense in a regular manner, some verbs are irregular and alter their form. As you know, many students pick up form changes automatically, but many others will require step-by-step explanations of forming tenses, especially irregular past tenses.

	Regular	**Irregular**
Present:	She plays.	She eats.
Past:	She played.	She ate.

Agreement between subject and verb also proves tricky for many students, so practice making subject and verb agree must also be built into verb-tense lessons.

Lesson

It Will Happen Already?

Label the chalkboard "Past," "Present," and "Future" (traditional time-line order), then hold a discussion about verb tense, explaining that when we speak we use verb tense to let the listener know when a story or event took place. And authors like to do the same in their writing. Using verb tense correctly lets people understand exactly what you mean when you speak or write.

Ask, *If I ask you to* retell *what happened to you, what tense will you use? And if I ask you to* predict *who will be elected president, what tense will you use?* Explain to the class that you will write short stories together right then at the chalkboard. Say, *I'll read a sentence, and let's see if you can figure out which tense I'm using. Then we'll continue the story for three sentences in the same tense.*

Here are three possible story-starter sentences:

> When I live on my own, I will own a
>   tremendous dog.
> I flew to California.
> I stare at the trees out the window.

Wrap-up

Explain to your students that correctly using verb tenses will let them sound as if they really know what they're talking about when they speak and write. Their conversation will be *persuasive* because it will be clear; their writing will be interesting. To demonstrate this, challenge students to rewrite the three group stories from the lesson in a way that bungles verb tense. Ask them to share their results and discuss whether they're confusing.

Use the group stories also to teach subject/verb agreement (you may want to save this for another time). Ask students to change all *singular* subjects and verbs to *plural*. Discuss the results.

Extension Activities

ORAL LANGUAGE

Gone, Coming, Going

Give each pair of students a photograph or picture from a magazine or newspaper that shows action. Explain that the picture has caught the present. For instance, if a photograph pictures a baseball player swinging a bat, say, *The baseball player* swings *the bat. The action is happening* now, *in the present, so we use the present tense to describe it. Before the player stepped to the plate, he* took *practice swings. That happened already; it's in the past, so we use the past tense to talk about it*, and so on.

Student pairs think up sentences in the present as captions for their pictures. Then each student will draw one of the missing "before" or "after" scenes and write the caption for that picture, in the correct tense. Display the results on the Writers' Wall.

ORAL LANGUAGE

I Came, I See, I Will Tell You All About It

Draw a time line on the chalkboard like the one below as a visual aid:

<u>past   present   future</u>

In small groups of three or four, students orally share two sentences about themselves using the past tense. Then they tell two sentences about themselves using the present tense and, finally, two sentences using the future tense.

(Note: This serves as a prewriting activity for "I Came, I See, I Will Write All About It," below.)

LITERATURE CONNECTION

Literature Connection

Compare texts that are written in the past and present tenses. Discuss why the author chooses that tense. Ask, *How does the story in the present tense make you feel?* Lead students to understand that the present tense may bring us into a story with a sense of intimacy and immediacy. Ask also, *How does the story in the past tense make you feel?* Try to elicit from students the idea that narrators of past-tense stories have already experienced what they're relating. Ask, *For what kinds of stories would you use the past tense? For what kinds would you use the present?*

Here are a few books written in the present tense:

Red Fox Running
by Eve Bunting, 1993, Clarion Books, NY

> Red fox running,
> Running through the snow,
> White sky above
> And the white earth below.
> Winter should be over,
> But it didn't go away,
> Hunger runs beside you
> On this cold and frozen day.

And So They Build
by Bert Kitchen, 1993, Candlewick Press, Cambridge, MA

This is a nonfiction book about 12 animals that build.

> A male satin bowerbird is looking for a mate and so he builds…
> Satin bowerbirds live in the rainforests of eastern Australia.

Sun Song
by Jean Marzollo, 1995, HarperCollins Publishers, NY

> Sun, light the woods
> With the soft spring dawn;
> Shine on the spots
> Of a newborn fawn.

Like Butter on Pancakes by Jonathan London, 1995, Puffin Books, NY

> First light melts
> like butter on pancakes,
> spreads warm and yellow
> across your pillow.

The following book from the Clarion Word

Play series plays with irregular verbs:
I Think I Thought: And Other Tricky Verbs
by Marvin Terban, 1984, Clarion Books, NY

Flamingo **flies** to Florida with her daughter.
Flying fish **flew** right out of the water.

I Came, I See, I Will Write All About It

Invite students to write out their time-line stories from "I Came, I See, I Will Tell…"

I See in Your Future…

Students can write single-sentence predictions about their classmates. (Remind them that the predictions must be positive.) They begin with the classmate's present and then predict what will result in the future.

Because Tommy knows all the constellations, he will discover a new star and name it for himself.

Wheels Today, Anti-Gravity Packs Tomorrow

Students choose an invention and talk about how people did without it in the past (or what was used in its place), how we use the invention now, and how this invention may change or become obsolete in the future.

In the past, pioneers used a fire to keep warm.

Today, we have central heating, although we build fires because we like to watch them.

In the future, everyone will have solar panels, which will store solar power and be more efficient than today's heaters.

Writers' Wall

Post the "Gone, Coming, Going" pictures with their captions. Also post any "tricky" verbs so they will be visible for editing purposes.

Combination: Nouns, Adjectives, Verbs

Student Objective

To build sentences by combining nouns, adjectives, and verbs.

Lesson

Putting Them All Together

Now that your students have examined the basic elements of sentences, it's time for them to see how those elements combine to form sentences and to practice combining the elements themselves.

Create sentences with parts missing or use *Wacky Mad Libs* by Roger Price and Leonard Stern (Scholastic Inc., 1991). Choose stories that are appropriate for the age of students you work with. Students will love hearing the funny stories that result from the words they fill in.

The Three Little Pigs

Once upon a time there were three little pigs who decided to build themselves houses. The first pig was _moldy_ (adjective), and he built his house out of _gerbils_ (plural noun).

Wrap-up

Explain to students that a sentence has to have a noun and a verb, a subject to do (or be) something and the action that the subject is doing (or being). Show them the most basic kinds of sentences, such as *She runs* or *I am*. Then show them that adjectives can be added to some basic sentences to make them slightly more expressive—*Anita is tall*, for instance.

Ask students if the explanation makes sense; challenge them to demonstrate writing such basic sentences. Some students may figure out that adverbs can also turn the most basic sentences into slightly more expressive ones.

Extension Activities

Pass-Around Squares

Give each group of four students a square that has its center point marked. Let one student fold each corner to the center point and mark each flap consecutively *article, adjective, singular noun, verb*. Another student then opens each flap and writes the numbers one to four.

Now the square with the flaps down is passed to a new student. That student opens the first flap, writes an article, closes the flap, and passes the square to the next student. That student, without looking at what the previous student wrote, opens the next flap and writes an adjective; then he or she passes the square to the next student, who writes a singular noun under the next flap, and so on. When the first round is finished, all flaps are opened and the sentence is read; the numbers on the flaps indicate the order in which the words should be read.

Students take turns recording the sentences in a numbered list.

You might want to brainstorm articles, sometimes referred to as *determiners*. Appropriate ones for singular nouns are: *my, your, our, one, the, this, that, a, an,* and so on.

Sharon Shears Sheep in Sheds and Shacks

Students can work in pairs or small groups to write tongue twisters. Each pair or group thinks of a blend or a digraph. The students then brainstorm nouns, verbs, and adjectives beginning with that combination of letters. Encourage the use of a dictionary. When they have settled on six to ten words for each part of speech, students can write their own tongue twisters. Get students' creative juices flowing by reading them published tongue twisters. (Charles Keller's *Tongue Twisters* [see below] is just one of many books you might use.)

SH

NOUNS	VERBS	ADJECTIVES
Sharon	shouts	shy
showers	shakes	shaky
shells	shivers	sure
shore	shears	sharp
shed	shares	sheer
shack	shops	shallow
sheep	shuffles	shrewd
shark	shudders	showy

Sharon shears sheep with sharp shears in sheds and shacks.

Literature Connection

Tongue twisters and alliterative text are fun ways to illustrate that sentences are combinations of nouns, verbs, and adjectives.

Goblins in Green
by Nicholas Heller, 1995, A Mulberry Paperback Book, NY
(The pictures add a lot to the text.)

Selwin is sporting sorrel trousers.
Thompson is trying some tulip underwear,
while Ulrika unlooses her unusual veil.
Vincent looks vile in his violet woolies.

Tongue Twisters
by Charles Keller, 1989, Simon & Schuster
Books for Young Readers, NY

Spiral-shelled sea snails shuffle in sea shells.

Books That Build on Bold Connections

Using *Goblins in Green* as their model, students choose a proper noun and then a present tense verb beginning with the same letter. Next, they choose an adjective and a second noun that the adjective will modify; the adjective begins with the same letter as the first two words, but the noun begins with the next letter of the alphabet. Students might stay with monsters as a theme or choose another one. Groups of four or five students might write their own alliterative books on chosen themes.

Cinquains

A *cinquain* is a five-line verse that follows a strict syllable pattern; for this lesson, our cinquains will also require using certain parts of speech at each line:

1) noun: two syllables
2) two adjectives: four syllables
3) three participles: six syllables
4) a complete sentence: eight syllables
5) a noun that renames the noun of line one: two syllables

If some students are overly concerned about or stymied by counting syllables, invite them to ignore the restriction. The poems can be written about a character in literature, the student, a theme of study, a friend, a family member, and so on. (The cinquains can be arranged on the page as the author chooses.)

Lion
Strong, muscular,
Stalking, eating, sleeping.
Mother raises cubs expertly.
Hunter

Diamantes

Another type of poetry that makes use of combinations of parts of speech are diamantes (see "You Can"t See or Touch Them, but They're Things" on page 18 for a description of the diamante form).

City
Concrete, loud
Steaming, crowding, bustling
Freeways, traffic, lanes, pastures,
Cooling, relaxing, ambling,
Verdant, quiet
Country

Writers' Wall

You can, of course, post any of the finished projects on the Wall; it may be especially useful as a reference, and also fun for the students, to post the results from the "mad libs."

Adverbs

Student Objective

To understand that adverbs tell how, when, or where an action is done.

Background

The word *adverb* is derived from the Latin for "to or toward the word," because the adverb's function is to modify a verb, adjective, or other adverb, thus *adding to* another word's meaning. We add adverbs to tell us *how* something was done (He threw *hard*), *when* something was done (They played *yesterday*), or *where* something was done (She sat *nearby*). Many adverbs end in *ly* (They talked *rapidly*), but as the examples show, many others do not. So it is important to understand the adverb's function. However, the role of the adverb can be a tricky concept; practicing using adverbs is really the best way to understand what they are.

The examples above are of adverbs modifying verbs; the lesson gives examples of adverbs modifying adjectives and other adverbs.

Lesson

How (and When and Where) Do You Do?

Up, Up and Away (Grosset & Dunlap, 1991) by Ruth Heller presents myriad adverbs doing all the things adverbs can do. Read from the book and choose a selection to work with, or write the following quotation on the chalkboard:

> This cat is RATHER corpulent,
> and VERY soft and purry.

> She seems EXTREMELY confident and
> MORE than SOMEWHAT furry.
> She's TOO well-fed,
> and SO well-bred, ornamental quadruped.

Discuss the roles of the adverbs that describe the cat. Explain that we know they're adverbs because of what other sorts of words they *modify*. *Rather*, for instance, tells us a little bit more about how *corpulent* the cat is, and *corpulent* is an adjective.

Now write a verb, such as *speak*, and challenge students to think of pairs of adverbs that describe *speak* oppositely. The idea is to create an opposite-adverbs "word mirror." For example:

slowly

softly   seldom

SPEAK

loudly   frequently

quickly

Wrap-up

Let students come up with their own "adverb mirrors" around verbs of their choice. They can make other opposite ones or adverb-synonym mirrors. Challenge them to think up non-ly adverbs.

Extension Activities

ORAL LANGUAGE

Adverb Interrogation

List the adverbs students thought of for the lesson. If the class made only one word mirror, have them brainstorm other adverbs. Choose one person to leave the room, then have the rest of the class pick one of the adverbs from the list. The person who is "it" returns to the room and must ask no more than five questions to determine which adverb was picked. Model the game first by asking, *If I spoke the adverb's way, would I be angry? Would I be happy?*

Swiftly, Tom Swifties

Have students create "Tom Swifties." A Tom Swifty uses an adverb that plays on the subject of the sentence, such as:

> "What a beautiful piece of wood," he said craftily.
> "I'll win the race," she said hurriedly.

Show and Tell

Challenge students to think up captions that include adverbs for pictures of your choice (*Action Alphabet* by Shelley Rotner is a great source for pictures). A caption for one of the pictures in *Action Alphabet* might read, *The boys tug forcefully.*

Literature Connection

Below are books that feature adverbs:

A Snake is Totally Tail
by J. Bennett, 1983, Macmillan Publishing Company, NY

> A kangaroo is partially pocket.
> A crocodile is mostly mouth.
> A dinosaur is entirely extinct.

The Maestro Plays
by Bill Martin Jr., 1970, Harcourt Brace & Company, NY

> The maestro plays.
> He plays proudly.
> He plays loudly.

Alliteratively Speaking

Challenge students to write alliterative sentences in which an adjective, a noun, a verb, and an adverb all begin with the same letter.

> Angry anteaters agitate awkwardly.
> Busy beavers build boldly.

The Many Ways of...

Using *The Maestro Plays* as a model, students choose their own subjects (a cook, a football player, a dancer, a monkey, and so on), and then string adverbs to modify verbs that describe what the subject does. Students then illustrate their sentences, providing a context for the adverbs.

> A cook bakes messily, rapidly, furiously, worriedly, busily, wonderfully.

Formally a Poem

Invite students to write an adverb poem in the following form:
Adverb
Adverb
Adverb
Noun Phrase
Verb
Prepositional Phrase

Here's a sample adverb poem.

Carelessly,
Recklessly,
Heedlessly,
The beginning skier
Careened
Down the slope.

Writers' Wall

Post any of the writing completed for this section. Also, after discussing uses of adverbs in student readings, post the verb/adverb pairs that you all agree are effective.

Pronouns

Student Objective

To understand the function of pronouns and using them to avoid repetition.

Background

Pronouns take the place of nouns or noun phrases, and because nouns do many things in sentences, there are many types of pronouns. For instance, personal pronouns can be divided into two classes: *subject* and *object*. Subject pronouns, as you might expect, take the place of the subject of a sentence (*I, you, he, she, it, we, you* (plural), *they*). Object pronouns take the place of the objects of verbs or prepositions (*me, you, him, her, it, us, them*). Possessive pronouns show ownership (*my, mine, your(s), his, her(s), our(s), their(s)*), and interrogative pronouns ask a question (*who, whom, which*). And there are other kinds as well (*demonstrative, indefinite, reflexive,* and *intensive*), which we use every day but don't think about technically.

While students of course also use pronouns in their speech, they do need to be taught to use pronouns in writing to avoid repetition. (And discussing *why* we don't like repetitive writing should really involve a discussion of the aesthetics of writing—beautiful language enthralls the reader, conveys the author's subject with authority [pun intended], and is, well, *beautiful* [a value in itself]. Asking students what kind of language is beautiful should also provoke an energetic debate.)

Lesson

Stand-Up Stand-ins

Pronouns are versatile, serving as they do in

place of people, things, places, and ideas. Introduce a lesson about them by letting students read Mary O'Neill's "Pronouns" (below). After two readings, ask for an explanation of what pronouns are, based on the poem, assisting students to adjust their understanding as necessary with the definition discussed above.

Pronouns

You're using a pronoun
When you refer
To anyone as:
Him, His, or Her,
A Who or a Whom
Or a He or a She,
A They or a Them,
A You or a Me.
But the one you'll use most
Is a two-letter bit—
The popular, marvelous,
Lazybone: IT!

Wrap-up

Ask students if they know, or can figure out, the difference between *he* and *him* and *who* and *whom*. Help them to see that one form is for subjects, and the other is for objects of verbs or prepositions. Thus we say, Whom *we elect matters* and *Serve the cake to* him.

Some students may recognize that *her* serves double duty as both a possessive and an object pronoun. And *you*, of course, stands in for singular and plural, subject and object nouns.

Extension Activities

ORAL LANGUAGE

She Did That to Her, But He Saw Her Do It

Give each pair of students a picture of

a scene with people interacting. Do not use pictures of a specific character, like Superman or Aladdin. Instead, use pictures of characters students can give names to. Then let the pairs present to the class their versions of what's happening in the pictures. They will naturally use pronouns. Ask a student to act as secretary and silently record the pronouns each pair uses. Once in a while, challenge a pair to repeat the story without using a single pronoun, or using only pronouns. These exercises will require concentration and point out to the speakers and the audience the repetitiousness of always using names and the vagueness of using only pronouns.

ORAL LANGUAGE — Pronouns Free Nouns From Word Cluster

Make a 24-word cluster. In each of 24 shapes, write a noun or pair of nouns. Students connect two shapes (from anywhere in the constellation of shapes) with a line, then write a sentence using those nouns. After they write the sentence, they rewrite it, changing the nouns to pronouns.

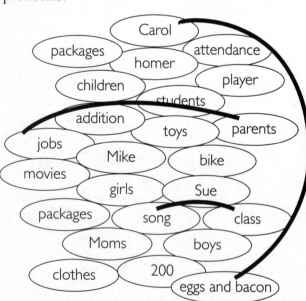

With the model figured here, the following sentences could be made:

> Carol likes eggs and bacon.
> *She likes them.*
> Parents like jobs.
> *They like them.*
> Our class liked composing a song.
> *We liked composing it.*

ORAL LANGUAGE — Tracking Them, It, and Others

Read *The Funny Little Woman* (see below) to the class. Then read it again, and have students keep track of all the pronouns used in the story. Students share their lists in small groups. Then each group constructs four sentences about the story using the pronouns they listed.

LITERATURE CONNECTION — Literature Connection

Any book is suitable for discussing to whom or what pronouns refer. Here are some picture books that can help students see that using only nouns would be repetitious:

The Funny Little Woman
by Arlene Mosel, 1972, E.P. Dutton, NY

> "Tee-he-he-he," laughed the little woman as the wicked oni took her down the road to a wide river. He put her into a boat and took her across the river to a strange house.

Miss Rumphius
by Barbara Cooney, 1982, The Trumpet Club, NY

> The next spring Miss Rumphius was not very well. Her back was bothering her again, and she had to stay in bed most of the time. The flowers she had planted the summer before had come up and bloomed in spite of the stony ground. She could see them from her bedroom window, blue and purple and rose-colored.

Biography Riddles

Challenge students to write a biography riddle, which describes a person using only pronouns. The reader tries to guess the name of the person. Characters in books you are reading are also great for this activity. Here is a biography riddle for a character:

> She has the worst-behaved students in the entire school. They are surprised when she doesn't show up for school one day. Her substitute is Miss Swamp, who is mean. Her class is happy when she returns.

Answer: *Miss Nelson from Miss Nelson is Missing!* by Harry Allard (Houghton Mifflin Company, 1972).

Writers' Wall

Record and display captions from "She Did That to Her, But He Saw Her Do It." Also, post "Pronouns" (above) so that students can use it as a definition and example reference.

Prepositions

Student Objective

To understand the role of prepositions.

Background

Prepositions define the relationship between nouns, pronouns, or nouns and pronouns. They are often "positional words," indicating actual physical positions of things, or figurative positions. In fact, a useful way to introduce to the class the idea of prepositions is to talk about an object, say a book, in relation to something larger, such as the teacher's desk. Put the book on the desk and announce, *On the desk.* Move the book all around the desk, announcing its position each time, pointing out that the positional words are *prepositions.*

Explain that prepositions usually show up in sentences as parts of phrases, *prepositional phrases,* which include a preposition, an object of the preposition (a noun or pronoun that comes after the preposition), and articles or descriptives that come in between. Write examples on the chalkboard; for each, explain which is the preposition, which its object, and what the prepositional phrase is. Below, the italicized word is the preposition, the boldface word its object, and the underlined words the prepositional phrase:

> A child hid *in* the **tree**.
> A second child hid *near* the **bushes**.
> The third child hid *behind* the red **barn**.

Lesson

In, Around, and About Prepositions

Read the class *Rosie's Walk* by Pat Hutchins (Scholastic, 1992). The entire book is one sentence long, linking prepositional phrase after prepositional phrase. On the first reading, have students keep track of where Rosie goes, which is told through prepositional phrases. On the second reading, have students record prepositional phrases for the antics of the fox.

Rosie the hen went for a walk
across the yard
around the pond
over the haystack…

Wrap-up

Ask, *Can you think of prepositional phrases that sound physical but don't literally mean that one thing is* under *or* over *or at the bottom of something else?* Explain that many prepositional phrases are *figurative* and explain *abstract* relations. Of course, this explanation will be less useful than actual examples, such as *under the weather, in the clouds, aboveboard*, and so on.

Extension Activities

Paint by Preposition

Give half of the students drawings of objects in various relations. These students pair up with the rest of their classmates, who have drawing paper and pencils. The pairs sit back to back. Students with the pictures give only oral directions by which their partners try to draw a similar picture. (Attribute blocks can be used instead of drawings.) Their directions should be rich in prepositional phrases:

> There's a circle in the middle of the paper. On the left of the circle, there's a square that's bigger than the circle. On top of the square, there's a small triangle. Under the circle is a skinny, long rectangle.

Up With Geography

Using maps (and this can be a language extension of a social studies segment), students choose destinations and then tell partners how to get there. For example, with a map of a zoo, the directing partner might say,

Put your finger on the park entrance sign, walk across the bridge, around the lake, through the cave, and you'll come to the Lion's Lair. Then partners switch roles. Of course, city and state maps work well, too.

Rolling Across and Down

This activity was developed by teacher Joni Troup.

Draw a six-square by six-square grid as shown below. In each square write a preposition. On one side and along the top of the grid, write a noun for each row and column (they can relate to topics of study, a book, a holiday, and so on). Students roll two dice, one at a time. The first die identifies a column, counting one through six from left to right. The second die identifies the square in the column. (Rolls of three and then five would land the player in the *on top of* square below.) The student then must make a sentence using the two words outside the grid and the preposition in the square. For example, *The pumpkin rested on top of the tree.*

	cat	monster	pumpkin	ghost	skeleton	scarecrow
broom	on	beside	under	above	through	with
window	behind	next to	around	off	over	across
fence	into	by	from	towards	near	under
porch	between	after	along	to	behind	against
tree	past	inside	on top of	before	down	by
attic	off	under	through	on	next to	in

Literature Connection

Simple picture books are great for presenting prepositions. Below are three:

Hide and Snake
by Keith Baker, 1991, The Trumpet Club, NY

> I'm looping through yarn,
> curling 'round hats,
> wrapping 'round presents, and napping
>   with cats.

Outside, Inside
by Carolyn Crimi, 1995, Scholastic Inc., NY

> Outside, tree leaves flap in the crying wind.
> Inside, Molly's slippers whisper down
>   the hall.
> Outside, a worried rabbit darts across the
>   lawn....

As the Crow Flies: A First Book of Maps
by Gail Hartman, 1993, Aladdin Paperbacks, NY

> AS THE EAGLE SOARS
> From the mountains, a stream flows
>   through a meadow
> where a tall tree stands.

Leading Readers Up, Down, and Around

Using *Rosie's Walk* as a model, students write stories about animals of their choice—for instance, a student could write a one-sentence-chain of prepositional phrases relating a lion stalking a zebra in the African savanna.

> Zeb the zebra didn't realize when he went for a walk that in the grass of the savanna, along the edge of the wood, between shrubs and bushes, over thorns, beside the river, Leon the lion was stalking him.

Prepositional Poem

Invite students to write a preposition poem in the following form:

Noun
Verb, verb, verb
Prepositional phrase
Prepositional phrase
Prepositional phrase
Noun

Here's a sample prepositional poem.

Snow
Blows, swirls, twirls
Over the rooftops,
Through the cracks,
Over all the globe—
Whirlwind!

Writers' Wall

A collection of prepositions will be helpful as students write their poems or stories. Have students add to this list by brainstorming or finding prepositions in their readings. Or include prepositions they thought of for any of the above activities. Here is a list to start with or for filling out the student list:

about	into
above	like
across	near
after	of
against	off
along	on
among	on top of
around	onto
at	out of
before	outside
behind	over
below	past
beneath	since
beside	through
between	to
by	toward
down	under
during	underneath
except	until
for	up
from	upon
in	with
inside	within
in front of	without
instead of	

Conjunctions

Student Objective

To understand that the role of conjunctions is to join parts of sentences.

Background

There are three types of conjunctions: coordinating (*and, or, but, nor, for, so, yet*); subordinating (*after, although, as, as long as, because, before, except, for, in case, since, so, so that, though, until, unless, when, whenever, where, whereas, while,* and so on); and correlative, which come in pairs (*either…or, neither…nor, both…and, not only… but, whether…or*). Studying conjunctions allows students to see the several ways there are to combine two statements while showing the relationship between them.

Lesson

Conjunctions' Functions

Start students thinking about conjunctions by writing out and reading Mary O'Neill's "Conjunctions." Let a volunteer or two read it aloud, then ask, *Did anyone ever think about these little words before? Could anyone try to explain to us what a conjunction is and what it does?* You will probably want to help students refine the definitions they come up with.

Conjunctions

A conjunction's the word
Between sister AND brother
That keeps them from running
Smack into each other.

A conjunction's a word
That adds to a thought:

"BUT I don't always do
The things that I ought!"

A conjunction's a word
That expresses a choice:
"I can whisper OR scream
With my only-one voice!"

Wrap-up

Challenge students to come up with sentences on the spot that use some of the more sophisticated conjunctions listed above. Lead them to articulate that some conjunctions can join only simple words while others join whole groups of words (of course, students don't need to understand technically that those groups of words are clauses or phrases).

Students will probably have trouble distinguishing the proper uses of the more formal conjunctions that they've had little or no experience reading or using in conversation.

Extension Activities

Play the Conjunction You're Dealt

Write a different conjunction on each of 10 to 12 cards for each small group of three or four students, or let the groups write their own cards. Players shuffle the cards and then take turns choosing them. They must read the conjunction aloud, and then use it in a complete sentence. This can be played for points, if you like.

since: Since I was seven, I've been taking karate.

Conjunction Swap

Give groups of students piles of cards. Each card should list three words. The task is to pick a card and then use all three words in a sentence with one of the conjunctions displayed on the Writers' Wall. The next player must use the same words from the card but a different conjunction from the Wall. The third player chooses a new card and a new conjunction; the fourth uses the same card and a new conjunction, and so on.

Cards might read: *train, delay, storm; teacher, lunch, recess; storm, fishing, trout;* and sentences, then, might read:

Player No. 1
Because of the storm, the train was delayed.

Player No. 2
The storm delayed our trip to the station, so we missed the train.

Literature Connection

Use a page from any current reading book to talk about why the author used the conjunctions he or she did. Isaacs's *Swamp Angel* (see page 13) is a good book to use for this—it's an exciting story, with vivid characters, that illustrates very well how conjunctions can coordinate actions and ideas about characters.

She hiked back ten miles from where she had landed, and the fight commenced once more. Swamp Angel and Tarnation finally grew so tired they fell asleep, but that didn't stop them….

Tarnation snored louder than a rockslide, while Angel snored like a locomotive in a thunderstorm.

It's Fun to Be a Lion, But...

Invite students to imagine that they are anyone or anything they choose, animate or inanimate. Ask, *What is it like to be what you've chosen? What do you like about being what you've chosen? What don't you like about it? What are the advantages, and what are the limitations?* Students then write about the benefits and drawbacks using conjunctions, such as *although, even though, though, rather than, whereas, while,* and so on.

Clamp After Gluing Until Dry

Challenge students to write directions for making something. The task is to use conjunctions, such as *after, before, since, until, when,* and *while,* so that every step is clear, and a stranger could make what is being described.

Writers' Wall

Post a list of conjunctions (which students will need for "Conjunction Swap"). You might want to display "Conjunctions" (above) as the heading for the list. Students can, of course, add conjunctions from their reading.

Names and Functions of PUNCTUATION

As with the parts of speech, punctuation should be taught not as a value in and of itself, but as a crucial element of writing intelligibly. Punctuation marks are a system of signposts that direct meaning and aid comprehension by telling a reader how to *hear* words on a page, as if the author had spoken. Without punctuation, meaning would become garbled. In fact, before starting this section is the perfect time to introduce students to the idea that writing assumes an *audience*: we write in order to convey ideas to readers, also known as *other real people*, and so we must take care to arrange our words and punctuate them so that those words are clear and mean what we want them to mean.

Periods

Student Objective

To understand that periods are necessary between initials and after abbreviations.

Background

Students usually learn by the first grade that periods end declarative and imperative sentences. If students forget to put periods in, a quick reminder is all that is needed. (More difficult for students is how to write a complete sentence. Often they put periods at the end of sentence fragments, or they forget about completing thoughts and write run-ons. For help with these problems, see the section on sentences.)

Students have more difficulty remembering that periods are used after abbreviations and between initials. This lesson teaches both functions of the period together.

Lesson

The Short-Form Period

Invite three or four students to write their initials on the chalkboard. Point out that periods belong, or were correctly written, after each letter. Now ask three or four students to write the initials for what they *wish* their names were. The class might enjoy guessing the desired names before the students reveal them. Explain that periods also end abbreviations of words. Say, *Whenever you see a bunch of letters that you can't read, and that are ended with a period, you're looking at an abbreviation.* Ask a group of students to come to the chalkboard and abbreviate *mister, doctor, avenue,* and so on. (Some students may not be familiar with these words or their abbreviations.)

Wrap-up

Using periods for initials and abbreviations may simply require practice and more practice to learn. But an idea that may help some students is that, in those cases, the periods tell readers *not* to pronounce the letters as they appear, but to *read* the letters as if they were a whole word.

Extension Activities

Initial Responses

Divide students into small groups. Each has a deck of cards of open-ended questions. Students take turns answering the questions by using their initials, in sequence, as the first letters of the words in their answer.

Why do you like winter?

Nancy W. Clarke (N. W. C.) answers, *I like winter because I got a **n**ew **w**inter **c**oat.*

Mark S. Browne (M. S. B.) answers, *I like winter because I like to **m**ake **s**now**b**alls.*

If this is too difficult, students may use only their first and last initials.

Right in the Middle the Whole Time

Pairs of students can work together to find a famous person's middle name. Students then write the person's full name, with the middle initial, on the left side of a page, and write both the middle name and a fake middle name on the right side. They also record two facts about the person, which may serve as memory-jogs and will add interest to the activity. Then groups compile a master list of names and initials, mixing up the middle initials down the right side. Pairs take turns providing two clues for their contributions to the other students, who try to guess whom the clues describe and what the person's middle initial is. A short master list might look like this:

Martin L. King	Brenda Edmond
Susan B. Anthony	Elizabeth Taliaferro
Booker T. Washington	Eudora Lawrence
Robert (Ted) E. Turner	Brownell Luther
Emily E. Dickinson	Theodore Edward

And clues might run:
He was a pastor at the Ebenezer Baptist Church in Atlanta. He was the leader of the Civil Rights Movement.

Courtesy Requires

Students can continue "Right in the Middle the Whole Time" by matching an abbreviated title (*Mr., Mrs., Dr., Ms., Jr.,* and so on) to each name. This may require further research.

Literature Connection

Below are two books that feature abbreviations in addresses:

Postcards From Pluto
by Loreen Leedy, 1993, Scholastic Inc., NY

> Mr. and Mrs. Chang
> 808 Circle Court
> Loopdeloop, CA
> U.S.A. 90287

Stringbean's Trip to the Shining Sea
by Vera B. Williams, 1988, Greenwillow Books, NY

> Mr. and Ms. Coe
> and Mr. F. M.
> Coe Springs Motel
> Jeloway, KS.
> 66708

(Note: The state abbreviation is incorrectly punctuated. There should be no period.).

Forging Ahead With Our Studies

Student pairs invent a quotation that a person researched for "Right in the Middle the Whole Time" could plausibly have said. The quotation must be related to the person's accomplishments. Teach students that quotations often appear, as does the fake one below, in the following format:

> A peaceful way settles disputes.
> Dr. Martin Luther King

Clerihews

Challenge students to write clerihews about famous people or themselves. The clerihew was invented by E. C. (E. *Clerihew*) Bentley, a British writer. Clerihews are four lines, the first and second, and the third and fourth, forming rhymed couplets, and they usually make rhyming jokes with names and words that relate to the subject. For this activity, require students to use the subject's name at the end of the first line. (Rhyming dictionaries may make this activity more enjoyable and exciting for many students.)

> **E. B. White**
> The writer E. B. White
> Turned an ordinary sight
> Of a web and a swine
> Into a literary gold mine.

Writers' Wall

Post famous people's initials and let students guess the whole names. Also, post fake quotations from "Forging Ahead With Our Studies."

Question Marks

Student Objective

To understand how to form interrogative sentences and end them with question marks.

Background

Students certainly know how to *ask* questions (and ask, and ask, and ask…), but they will also need to learn, or at least practice, the rules for writing them. This section will provide plenty of that practice through challenging and exciting activities. And students will do more than practice writing conventions—they will become journalists, investigators, mentors, and authors.

A fun way to start investigating interrogatives, emphasizing the need for question marks at the end of questions, is to contrast English use of the question mark with the Spanish use of it. In Spanish the question mark comes upside-down before the question and also rightside-up after the question. *Are There Any Questions?* by Denys Cazet (see Literature Connection in the exclamation mark lesson) includes the Spanish way of punctuating questions.

Lesson

Ten Questions

Copy O'Neill's "QUESTION MARK" and ask for volunteers to read it aloud. After two readings, discuss the necessary components of a question. Ask, *What do we always see in a question? What kinds of words do questions usually have?* Lead students to articulate that questions often include *who, what, when, where, why,* or *how,* and that they also often require inverting the usual

subject/verb order.

> Symbol of all I wish I knew
> Polka dot under a curlicue….

Wrap-up

Bring in several objects and paper bags to hide them in. Direct students to brainstorm a list of questions that might be effective for discovering what's in the bag. Point out the sorts of questions that might be successful, such as, *What color is it? Is it a toy? Is it breakable?* But students are allowed only ten questions per bag, so they must realize that the questions should build on each other. After each round, discuss the way the questions they asked were formed. (Of course, students will be eager to continue playing, so the post-round discussion will work best if it's brief and to the point.)

Extension Activities

Ten by Ten

Ask students to bring their own things from home, hidden in paper bags. Divide students into ten (or more, or fewer) small groups. For each round, one student acts as the teacher. Again, groups ask no more than ten questions and then must guess what's in the bag. To ensure that a bag's contents are secret, require groups to use the bags of students not in their group.

On the Spot

In small groups, each student writes three questions and passes the page to the right. Now students must answer the three surprise questions as inventively as they can.

Q. What's at the end of the rainbow?

A. At the end of rainbow is the cloud with the silver lining.

Q. Why can't I stay up late on school nights?

A. You can't stay up late because when your sleepy head falls on the desk, it will make a loud noise, waking up everyone else.

The Fundamental Questions of Journalism

ORAL LANGUAGE

Newspapers often provide a good look at questions. Have students choose short articles that interest them, or you choose articles ahead of time, finding enough that students will still have a choice. Glue the article onto a larger piece of paper and write *Who? What? When? Where? Why?* and *How?* around the article. Students must draw lines from each interrogative to the part of the article that answers the corresponding question. Students can present their article to the class by explaining its topic and answering the six questions.

(Note: First discussing the differences between the six interrogatives would probably help most students significantly.)

Literature Connection

LITERATURE CONNECTION

The following books explicitly pose questions and answer them (and the tables of contents are arranged by question and so will serve as models for "Question Picture Books," below):

Why is Soap Slippery? and Other Bathtime Questions
by Catherine Ripley, 1995, Owl Books, Toronto

How can hot and cold water run out of the same tap?

Ow! Why do some shampoos sting my eyes?

Why can I draw on the mirror?

I Wonder Why Romans Wore Togas and Other Questions About Ancient Rome

by Fiona Macdonald, 1997, Kingfisher, NY (one in a series of I Wonder Why books)

What language did Romans speak?

What did Roman children play with?

Why were Roman roads so straight?

What's in the News?

WRITING CONNECTION

Challenge students to work together to write newspaper articles that satisfy the six-question standard (per above). The articles should have a definite focus and be written as if the topics were important current events:

◆ a specific historical event in the news
◆ classroom activities in the news
◆ nursery or fairy tale characters in the news

Question Picture Books

WRITING CONNECTION

Students might enjoy writing personalized picture books for kindergartners or first graders using the question pattern found in many picture books. Arrange with a colleague to partner each student with a younger child. When partners meet, older students ask younger ones what theme or topics they're interested in and what questions they'd like answered on those subjects. After the interview, students write the text of their books, evaluate their peers' texts, and then revise their own texts, keeping in mind who the *audience* of the books is—their younger partners. (If you haven't set up a system of peer or teacher evaluation and revision, this project provides a great opportunity to do so.)

When the text is finished, student-authors can then illustrate their books. And when the final product is ready, the author-illustrators present the books to their younger partners, first reading the books to them and then reading them together. (Your students should be made aware that their partners may not be able to read yet, so the shared reading may go slowly.)

Finally, the older students present the books to the younger children to keep; this presentation can be as ceremonious or casual as you like.

Interview With Darrell Arrow on Dinosaurs

WRITING CONNECTION

Interview With a Poem

Challenge students to write question poems, using as a model "Sea-sand and

Sorrow" by Christina Rossetti.

Sea-sand and Sorrow

What are heavy? Sea-sand and sorrow:
What are brief? Today and tomorrow:
What are frail? Spring blossoms and youth:
What are deep? The ocean and truth.

WRITERS' WALL

Writers' Wall

Exhibit any of the products of this section's activities.

Exclamation Marks

Student Objective

To understand that exclamatory sentences show strong feelings and end in exclamation marks.

Background

Exclamation marks denote strong feeling and can be used not only at the end of a sentence (I won!) but after a word or phrase (*Yeah! Happy New Year! Rats!*). Since *emphasizing* is attractive to students, they do tend to overuse the exclamation mark. So teaching them proper use of the exclamation mark is important! As with teaching the question mark, starting off with the contrast between English and Spanish uses of the exclamation mark (which also appears upside-down and at the beginning of a Spanish exclamation) makes for a fun, memorable lesson.

Lesson

Exclaim It!

Copy O'Neill's "Exclamation Point" and ask for volunteers to read it aloud. After two readings, discuss the necessary components of an exclamation. Ask, *What do we always see in an exclamation? What kinds of words make exclamations? And what kinds of feelings require exclamation marks?* Lead students to articulate that exclamations express strong feelings, such as *excitement, anger, frustration, pleasure, surprise,* and so on.

Exclamation Point
At the end of a word or a line to excite,
Scare or command it is proper to write !

Wrap-up

Explain to students that exclamation marks need to be used judiciously. If writing is filled with them, it just sounds to the reader like shouting. The exclamation mark can be very effective, but to be so it needs to stand out.

Extension Activities

I'm Exclaiming

Have students brainstorm single words or phrases that convey strong feeling and need exclamation marks. Then ask them to express the same sentiments as sentences ending with exclamation marks; the sentences can start with one of the single words or phrases.

Help!	Yum!
Great!	Super!
Yuck!	Yeah!
Yes!	Absolutely!
Oh no!	Finally!

Help! The Loch Ness monster is giving me a ride!

We're All So Excited! Startled! Scared!

Small groups receive situation cards. Each group must work together to role-play the situation named on the card, and they must include a number of exclamations. Here are a few situations that require strong feelings:

◆ You are all at a picnic, and an army of ants marches across your food.
◆ You are all at a high school football game, and your star quarterback is running down the field toward an open end-zone.

◆ You are all contestants in an All-You-Can-Eat pizza contest. Ready, set, EAT!

Literature Connection

Selected below are four picture books that feature exclamation marks:

Are There Any Questions?
by Denys Cazet, 1992, Scholastic Inc., NY

This story makes use of speech balloons as well as narrative text. Some of the speech balloons show single word exclamations: WOW! STOP! OUCH! OUT!

Grandma and the Pirates
by Phoebe Gilman, 1990, Scholastic Inc., NY

> Yo, ho! Yum, yum! We smell noodles! We want some. Yo, ho! Yum, yum! Look out noodles, here we come!

The Crocodile and the Dentist
by Taro Gomi, 1984, Scholastic Inc., NY

> This is the tale of two points of view, a dentist's and a crocodile's. They say the same thing but mean something different.

> I *really* don't want to see him…but I must.
> I *really* don't want to see him…but I must.
> Aaugh!
> Aaugh!

Rhinos Who Snowboard
by Julie Mamma, 1997, Chronicle Books, San Francisco

> It is so UNCOOL
> when MOGUL hopping KOOKS
> botch up their big jumps.
> BUMMER!

What Color is Your Mood Ring?

Compare two books, one with exclamation marks and one without. Talk about how and why the moods differ. (Two such books with widely differing moods are *Jamberry* by Bruce Degan [HarperCollins Publishers, 1983] and *The Salamander Room* by Anne Mazer

[The Trumpet Club, 1991], the former being fun-loving and excited, the latter being calm and matter-of-fact.) Ask, *What parts of a story's language create the mood? What are the fast indicators of a story's mood, as if the story were wearing a mood ring?*

Allow students, working in pairs, to choose a situation. They first write a story about that situation using a lot of exclamation marks, and then they rewrite it using no exclamation marks in order to change the mood of the piece.

Speak Your Mind

Challenge students to write a persuasive paragraph that uses one exclamation mark to make a point. This paragraph should reflect a strongly held opinion about a specific topic.

Writers' Wall

Students can post one word exclamations and exclaiming sentences that they've written or found in their readings. You might want to exhibit the two versions of the stories written for "What Color is Your Mood Ring?" They may serve as concrete examples of the powers of punctuation and tone.

Commas in a Series

Student Objective

To understand that commas separate words in a series.

Background

Commas separate words in a series, such as a list of items, so that the writing is clear to readers. In fact, the need for serial commas is evident in most cases, so teaching their use in terms of keeping meaning clear, rather than in terms of a grammatical rule, enables most students to pick up the concept quickly (though, of course, practice will be necessary to turn concept into application).

Explain to students that two things in a list can be confused as one thing, so, as writers, we make it obvious that they're *two* things by writing a comma between them. Sometimes a comma isn't needed between the last two things in a series, but sometimes the meaning wouldn't be clear without that final comma, so we use it.

Write the following sentence on the chalkboard and say, *Here's a sentence that could use a final serial comma: Anna, Mary and Sally wrote me letters. Ask, How many letters did I receive? Did Anna write me a letter, or am I telling her about two letters from Mary and Sally? Or am I telling her about one letter written by both Mary and Sally? Or*

am I telling someone else about two letters, one written by Anna and one written by both Mary and Sally? If the context makes it clear that the speaker is addressing Anna, then the sentence means that both Mary and Sally wrote letters. If the speaker is not addressing Anna, then the sentence is not clear. But if it were meant to indicate that the speaker received three separate letters, then a serial comma would clear it up: *Anna, Mary, and Sally wrote me letters.*

Lesson

50% Pizza, 33% Hamburgers, and 17% Chocolate Pudding

Discuss the need for serial commas. Then have students take turns polling their peers at their table or in small groups. They should ask questions such as *What is your favorite cafeteria food? and restaurant food? What is your favorite book? and author?* Students write up their findings, making sure to punctuate the listed answers with the necessary commas.

> We had two people who said their favorite restaurant food was hamburgers, three people who said it was pizza, and one person who said chocolate pudding.

Wrap-up

Ask students if they understand when and where to place commas in sentences. Explain that using commas isn't a matter of guessing (since some students panic and throw them in anywhere), reiterating that commas are there simply to separate ideas and things so that a reader can understand the writing.

Extension Activities

Serial Comma Separates Cereal From Dime in Student Pocket

Students can devise a list from whatever they bring with them to class. In groups of four, have them empty their pockets and list the items they find there. When the lists are compiled, ask them to present the results. Explain that they can arrange the list in order of importance, interest, humor, and so on, and that the order can run least to most or most to least, as they choose. Also, lists have a rhythm; they should play around with the order to find the rhythm they like.

> We had a piece of candy, two dimes, and a plastic spider in our pockets.

> In his pocket he had a pencil, a safety pin, and a dehydrated blue lizard!

> Our table liked hamburgers, french fries, and a pizza with everything on it.

The Sum of Our Parts Equals...

Students work in small groups of three or four. Each student has five cards: On the first they write a person's proper name; on the second, something that person can do; on the third, the name of a singular animal; on the fourth, something the animal can do; and on the fifth, an article or possessive that completes the second simple sentence.

> card 1: Jimmy
> card 2: runs
> card 3 monkey
> card 4: climbs
> card 5: my

All the cards go in the middle of the table, and together the group attempts to make the longest sentence possible from their 15 or 20 words cards. To do this, they will need to use serial commas. Pass out blank cards on which students can write punctuation marks and one conjunction; they use these cards to punctuate their sentence. The game can be played for points; each card—word and punctuation— counts as one point. Of course, meaning must be apparent for complete points.

Literature Connection

Below are two books that especially feature serial commas:

My Mama Says There Aren't Any Zombies, Ghosts, Vampires, Creatures, Demons, Monsters, Fiends, Goblins, or Things
by Judith Viorst, 1973, The Trumpet Club, NY

Alexander and the Terrible, Horrible, No Good, Very Bad Day
by Judith Viorst, 1972, Atheneum, NY

Words, Words, and Words = String Poems

Many poets write *string poems*, and these can be used to practice commas in a series. Below is one by Mary O'Neill called "Sound of Water" from *What Is That Sound!* (Atheneum, 1966). Challenge students to write their own string poems. They might want to begin by listing words that come to mind when thinking about an event, person, or thing. In O'Neill's model, all the sound words are verbs, and many are onomatopoetic. If students have brainstormed their verbs on separate pieces of paper, they can move the scraps around until they like the sound of the string of words and then write their draft.

Sound of Water

The sound of water is:
Rain,
Lap,
Fold,
Slap,
Gurgle,
Splash,
Churn,
Crash,
Murmur,
Pour,
Ripple,
Roar,
Plunge,
Drip,
Spout,
Slip,
Sprinkle,
Flow,
Ice,
Snow.

Cats

Jumping,
Crawling,
Leaping,
Swirling,
Twisting,
Skidding,
Purring,
Napping.

Writers' Wall

Let students post interesting series they wrote for "Serial Comma Separates Cereal From Dime in Student Pocket" or that they find in their reading.

Commas for Appositives and Appositive Phrases

Student Objective

To recognize when to set off appositives or appositive phrases with commas.

Background

Appositives and *appositive phrases* are nouns or noun phrases that provide information about the subject of a sentence. They belong to the class Interrupters, which literally interrupt the course of a sentence; and they are equivalent to the subject grammatically. Thus, unless commonly associated with the subject, appositives and appositive phrases are set off from the subject by commas. They offer a way to expand and clarify a sentence, making it more interesting. For example, I might increase the relevance and interest of the sentence *Monique sprained her ankle* by adding an appositive that makes clear the seriousness of the injury: *Monique, the lead ballerina, sprained her ankle.*

Appositives and appositive phrases are not necessary to the grammar of the sentence (this is what being "equivalent" to the subject means). In other words, a sentence will still be intact and make perfect sense if an appositive or appositive phrase is removed; and the appositive or appositive phrase can also replace the subject, as would be the case for the unfortunate Monique: *The lead ballerina sprained her ankle.*

Lesson

Exclaim It!

Explain and illustrate for students what apposi-

tives are and that they must—again, unless commonly associated with the subject—be set off by commas. (In the sentence *The play* King Lear *is great,* for example, the play title is an appositive but need not be set off by commas. So it would also be correct to write *The great batter Sammy Sosa once…*) Then write a student's name on the chalkboard and invite the student to the front to complete a sentence about herself by adding a predicate.

    1) Stephanie
    2) likes to collect shells.

Choose another student to expand the sentence by adding a detail about the first student as an appositive.

    3) Stephanie, my best friend, likes to collect shells.

Ask another student to write a complete simple sentence on the chalkboard about a different student, and invite a fourth to come up and add an appositive to the new sentence. Ask throughout the process whether students have questions. (Some students may realize that other grammatical units can also interrupt a sentence and so should also be set off by commas.)

Wrap-up

Have students look through reading material to find examples of appositives and appositive phrases. In large print, they should copy the complete sentences they find onto strips for posting on the Writers' Wall. But first, when everyone has found an example, have the students collect the sentences into those that set off the appositive or appositive phrase with two commas and those that do it with one. Ask, *Why*

in some cases do we need two commas and in others only one? Lead students to articulate that some appositives interrupt sentences in the middle and others lead off or are tacked on to the end of sentences. (*Mark, the first baseman, hit a homer. A homer was hit by Mark, the first baseman.*)

Extension Activities

Just Let Me Squeeze in Here

Students can work with partners or in groups of three. Students write subject cards and predicate cards and then put them together to make sentences. Next, they expand the sentences by adding, on separate cards, an appositive or appositive phrase. Have comma and period cards available for each group. At the end, let the groups share their favorite two sentences.

Jan pitched.
Jan, a sixth grader, pitched.

Active Life With Appositive

Working in groups of three or four, students create casts of characters. (Pictures or photographs of people can help get creative juices flowing.) Students name their characters and then write a one-sentence sketch for each, using appositives. If you choose, students can also use people or characters from literature you are studying as subjects for their sentences.

Bob, a hard-working mechanic, discovers a bag containing $600,000,000.
Sarah, a tall and plain woman, loved to sing.

Literature Connection

There aren't many picture books that use appositives. Here are a few:

Miss Rumphius
by Barbara Cooney, 1982, The Trumpet Club, NY

One day she met the Bapa Raja, king of a fishing village.

Up North in Winter
by Deborah Hartley, 1986, Puffin Unicorn Books, NY

When Grandma's cow, Snow White, stopped giving milk, even that old cow ended up in the soup pot.

Brave Irene
by William Steig, 1986, Farrar, Straus & Giroux, NY

Mrs. Bobbin, the dressmaker, was tired and had a bad headache, but she still managed to sew the last stitches in the gown she was making.

Stretch Skits

Have students choose four characters from their sketches for "Active Life With Appositive" and write short skits about them.

Appropriate Appositives

Invite students to choose comic strips and describe the action in their own words. Each character in the comic strip must be identified by an appositive or appositive phrase at the character's first appearance.

Charlie Brown, the forlorn pitcher, is standing on the mound trying to get his team involved in the game.

At home plate Lucy, the loudmouthed catcher, walks out to the mound to confer with Charlie Brown.

Appositives Clean Up the Page

Relate coming up with appropriate appositives to sentence combining. Students can combine sentences from their skits, sketches, or reading by compacting one sentence into an appositive in the middle of another sentence. The test for creating a proper appositive or appositive phrase is whether they can remove it afterward and still have a grammatical sentence.

Before: Susan was a student. She was also a concert pianist.

After: Susan, a student, was also a concert pianist. Or: Susan, a concert pianist, was also a student.

Writers' Wall

Exhibit the sentences written for "Appositives Clean Up the Page."

Commas in a Compound Sentence

Student Objective

To understand that two independent clauses joined by a conjunction must be separated by a comma.

Background

Two complete sentences can, of course, be joined into one compound sentence with a conjunction, but those two distinct parts must be separated by a comma. If what follows the conjunction is not a sentence, no comma is needed.

Another way to think about it (and this will clue students in to what they should look for) is that if the grammatical parts on either side of the conjunction have a subject, then those parts must be separated by a comma. And if there is only one subject in the first part of the sentence (the conjunction acting as a hinge between the two parts), then a comma is not appropriate. So we would write *I like vanilla ice cream, but she*

likes chocolate because both parts of the compound sentence have a subject (*I* and *she*). But we would write *I like vanilla but not chocolate* because the sentence has only one subject (*I*).

Lesson

Explain to students that writers often like to combine short sentences into longer ones so that their writing will not be repetitious and will sound mature and intelligent. Remind them that their basic goal as authors is to write pieces that attract readers, hold their attention, and, often, persuade them that the ideas expressed in the piece are right. So it is very important that they learn to write with authority!

Tell the class, *We can combine two sentences by joining them with a conjunction, but we have to separate the two halves of the new sentence with a comma, which comes in front of the conjunction.* Show students the following sentences and ask a volunteer to combine them at the chalkboard:

My students are wonderful. They are so smart. The volunteer may need some help arriving at the following: *My students are wonderful, and they are so smart.*

Now explain to the class that there's another way to combine two sentences, but this second way requires cutting words and not using a comma. Show them this version of the combined sentences: *My students are wonderful and smart.* Ask, *Can you see the difference between this way of combining them and the first way? What do you think the rule about when to use a comma and when not to use one might be?* Show students that when both halves do have subjects, then they must be separated by a comma and a conjunction. When one half keeps the subject and the other loses it, then a comma is *not* used. (Some students may be ready for the idea that two *sentences* require a comma and a conjunction while a sentence and *phrase* do not.)

Wrap-up

Invite students to the chalkboard to turn simple sentences into compound sentences and sentences with compound subjects and/or verbs. Provide them with sample sentences, or let them make them up on the spot. You will probably have to model use of coordinating conjunctions, as seen below.

> I will feed my dog, but I won't walk him. (compound sentence)
>
> I will feed my dog but won't walk him. (compound verb)
>
> Either I or my brother will feed the dog. (compound subject)

Extension Activities

Do the Compound Shuffle

Give student groups topics; these can be related to a unit of study. Groups then write six simple sentences about the topic on strips, which they cut up into separate words for some old-fashioned word processing. Give students comma and conjunction cards. Students try to combine two or more of their simple sentences by arranging them into a single compound sentence.

Before: Coral reefs are interesting.
Coral reefs are made from millions of animals called coral.
Corals have skeletons.
They attach to one another to make up a colony.
Colonies of coral make a reef.
Many creatures live in a reef.

After: Corals attach to one another to make colonies, and these colonies make up a reef.
Coral reefs are interesting, for many creatures live in a reef.

Sam You Are, But I Am Not

Challenge students to turn simple sentences from "early reader" books by Dr. Seuss into compound sentences. Have students use the homemade word processor method again. Ask, *Would more complex sentences make these books more challenging for young children? What do you think of the rewritten text?* Sometimes simple is better.

Before: I could not, would not, on a boat. I will not, will not, with a goat.

After: I could not, would not, on a boat, or I will not, will not, with a goat.

from *Green Eggs and Ham* by Dr. Seuss (Random House, Inc., 1988)

Other books suitable for this activity are the George and Martha series by J. Marshall and the Frog and Toad series by Arnold Lobel.

Literature Connection

Many picture books written for older students have compound subjects and verbs as well as compound sentences. Here are two:

Box Turtle at Long Pond
by William T. George, 1989, The Trumpet Club, NY

> The turtle opens his jaws and lunges, but the grasshopper jumps away.

Armadillo Rodeo
by Jan Brett, 1995, Scholastic Inc., NY

> Bo tried to catch sight of that rootin'-tootin' red armadillo, but he had to move fast.

Wishes, Lies, and Dreams

Take a lead from Kenneth Koch (*Wishes, Lies, and Dreams*, Harper & Row, 1970) and have students write poems which follow the form below. Remind them that if they write compound sentences, they have to include the comma; compound subject or verb sentences do not need the comma.

I seem to be _____,
but really I am _____.
I used to think _____,
but now I know _____.

Reshuffle Your Compounds

Students can use the facts generated for "Do the Compound Shuffle" to write an expository paragraph.

Writers' Wall

Post conjunctions that can be used to connect two independent clauses. And post sentences students admire, that they either wrote or found in their readings.

Quotation Marks

Student Objective

To understand that quotation marks enclose words spoken.

Background

Children love to write dialogue, and so it is necessary that we teach them the conventions of punctuating speech, though some of the rules are tricky for them. Generally, students are quick to pick up the concept of indicating spoken words with opening and closing quotation marks, beginning every quotation with a capital letter, and beginning a paragraph every time the speaker switches. But coordinating other punctuation with quotation marks gives many students trouble, especially since placement of punctuation depends on circumstance.

Commas, for instance, may come outside quotation marks (if a speaker tag precedes the quotation) or inside (if the tag follows the quotation): *The student said, "I don't get this." Or: "I don't get this," said the student.* Question and exclamation marks go *inside* quotation marks if the quotation itself is a question or exclamation:

"Why do I need to know this stuff?" asked the student. If the overall sentence is a question or exclamation, though the quotation is not, then the question or exclamation mark goes *outside* the quotation marks: *Did he say, "I'll never use this stuff in real life"?* A final point: If *both* the overall sentence and the quotation are a question or exclamation, then the question or exclamation marks go *inside* the quotation marks: *Did he say, "Why do we have to learn this stuff?"* Here are exclamation examples of the above:

> "Grammar!" he shouted.
> Don't whine, "Are we doing grammar?"!
> Don't say, "I hate grammar!"

Of course, quotation marks serve other functions: introducing new or unfamiliar words; emphasizing words as ironic; and identifying story, poem, chapter, article, and television show titles. But since children seldom use quotation marks for these reasons, they aren't addressed here.

Lesson

General Quoting

Discuss the rules of punctuating quotations, writing examples on the chalkboard and asking for volunteers to come up and invent their own examples. Then assign the following task: using any literature book with dialogue, students are to work in pairs to find patterns of quotation mark punctuation. Give them templates of a pattern to look for, such as "_____," _____. Then the pairs figure out other patterns and record them.

"_____?" _____.

_____, "_____."

"_____."

Wrap-up

Hold a discussion about the punctuation-of-quotation rules. Let students try to articulate the rules for themselves. Then post clear examples of the templates (student work, if it's clear enough) on the Writers' Wall, so the class has a visual reference for the rules.

Extension Activities

And You Can Quote Me On That!

Students brainstorm questions they want to ask classmates. Then pair them and let them interview each another, each asking four or five questions. The interviewer is required to take down the speaker's exact words to two responses. When both students have been the interviewer, group the pairs in threes (so each group is six students); students introduce their partners to the group based on the interviews. Afterward, ask how the interviews went (students, of course, will be more interested in the interchanges than in punctuating quotations). Ask, *Was it difficult to record the interviewee's exact words?* Explain that journalists and professional interviewers often use tape recorders so they can be sure of quoting their subjects exactly without slowing down the conversation. Then go over their quotation punctuation.

As I Am Fond of Saying...

Students imagine they are famous and might be quoted by the press at any moment. Ask, *What would you like to be known for having said?* Have students accurately write out their quotation as if it were excerpted from a newspaper. (This can also be expanded into a writing activity: have students write whole imaginary interviews with themselves.)

Literature Connection

Below are two books which tell their stories through dialogue only:

The Salamander Room
by Anne Mazer, 1991, The Trumpet Club, NY

> "Where will he sleep?" his mother asked. "I will make him a salamander bed to sleep in…"

The Day Jimmy's Boa Ate the Wash
by Trinka Hakes Noble, 1980, Dial Books for Young Readers, NY

> "How was your class trip to the farm?" "Oh…boring…kind of dull…until the cow started crying."

Readers Theatre

Have students create Readers Theatre scripts from short, simple storybooks, like Marshall's George and Martha series or Lobel's Frog and Toad series, or his *Fables* (HarperCollins, 1980). Then the young company can perform their works to kindergartners or first graders. Groups of students choose a story or fable; photocopy their selections so each student has the text. Students list the characters involved, possibly including one or two narrators (each student should have a role). The players underline or highlight their parts (point out that this is what professional actors do to learn their lines). Anyone playing a narrator gets to decide, maybe with some discussion, what background information must be told to move the story along. Each group should practice together until it can perform the play smoothly. The main object for the performers is to bring the characters to life by reading their lines (quotations!) with the appropriate meaning. There is no need for scenery, costumes, or props; Readers Theater productions are easy to perform.

Words of Wisdom

Have students collect quotations that they like, copying them out precisely. When they're done, ask them which pattern the quotations follow. Make books of quotations available for students. Some good ones are: *Incredible Quotations* by Jacqueline Sweeney (Scholastic, Inc. 1997); *Who Said That?: Famous Americans Speak* by Robert Burleigh (Henry Holt and Company, 1997); and *Shoptalk: Learning to Write With Writers* by Donald Murray (Heinemann, 1990). Murray's book contains quotations from well-known authors about the process of writing. Here's one for the Writers' Wall:

> Robert Anderson says, "A lot of writers wait for inspiration. The inspiration only hits you at the desk."

Putting Words in Their Mouths

Invite students to choose a comic strip and rewrite the story as a dialogue. Challenge students to use two or three different quotation patterns.

Writers' Wall

Post the quotation punctuation patterns so students have clear visual references. You may also want to exhibit the imaginary quotations students make up for themselves.

Dialogue Tags

Student Objective

To understand the need to vary verbs in dialogue tags.

Background

The last lesson assumed the *speaker tag* would be familiar. If it wasn't, it was probably obvious that *tag* refers here to the words that identify the speaker of a quotation. They come before or after the quotation and can also indicate *how* the speech is spoken. Adverbs and prepositional phrases are often part of the tag.

Students need to learn to vary the verbs they use in their dialogue tags. Otherwise, as we've all seen, their stories become masses of *he said/she said*. But at the same time that we encourage students to vary the verbs and find vivid, precise ones, we also have to warn them against *never* using *said*. *Said* is comfortable for the reader; it doesn't take attention away from the character's speech; and for certain frank or understated statements, it's the best choice. Also, we've all read student work that sounds more like a thesaurus than a story. While practicing using all available verbs is how students naturally learn to find the right ones, we can help them choose just the right word for the situation.

However, when we want to add volume and tone, we need new words. Instead of *said* we can use *whispered*, *shouted*, or *murmured*. Instead of *said* we can use *wept*, *sighed*, or *giggled*.

Lesson

Tag! You're Speaking

Explain to the class that since they already know how to write quotations, it time to learn how to write dialogue tags. See if students can articulate what *dialogue tags* are. Then discuss the need for alternating between the familiar *said* and other verbs that describe more precisely or flamboyantly *how* the speaker is speaking. Lead the class to articulate that the tags can convey tone, emotion, and behavior. Then, before breaking into groups for the lesson's task, model a well-written dialogue, from any book you choose, that uses both old standbys (*said*) and more descriptive tags (*shrieked*).

Have students work in pairs to come up with sample conversations between two people. This can be done orally: One person says the spoken words, and the other says the dialogue tag.

Student 1: "I don't want to go to the baseball game,"

Student 2: groaned Gloria.

Wrap-up

Let each group share a line or two from their sample conversations. Discuss whether the tags are successful. Of course, students will be eager to show off their knowledge of fancy words, which is fine. They'll have plenty of chances to practice varying their verbs.

Extension Activities

Tagging Verbs for Research

Give students a variety of books to look through from which they can copy down dialogue tags. But tell them they may write down only one tag for each verb (so they'll only have one example using *said*). Students then share their finds, and the class discusses why the various verbs were used—what tone, feeling, or simultaneous action the speech tags mean to convey

ORAL LANGUAGE — Tag Rummage

Record the specimens found for "Tagging Verbs for Research" on cards or scraps and put them in a hat or bag. Students think up short bits of dialogue (or take them from books) and read them in the manner directed by whatever tag they pull out of the hat. The speech might be as simple as *I want to go home*, and the tag could be *said Sal slowly, he whispered, Tom cried, Sue stammered,* or *Elton crowed!*

LITERATURE CONNECTION — Literature Connection

The first book presents a variety of verbs in tags but also weaves dialogue and narrative so tags are not always necessary:

John Henry
by Julius Lester, 1994, Dial Books, NY
[font]

> The next day the boss arrived with the steam drill. John Henry said to him, "Let's have a contest. Your steam drill against me and my hammers."
>
> The man laughed. "I've heard you're the best there ever was, John Henry. But even you can't outhammer a machine."
>
> "Let's find out," John Henry answered.
>
> Boss shrugged. "Don't make me no never mind...."

The next two books showcase dialogue without tags. Ask students how readers know who's talking. You might want to let them experiment by copying out the dialogue and adding tags (or photocopy it for them).

The Salamander Room
by Anne Mazer, 1991, Alfred A. Knopf, NY

> "Where will he sleep?" his mother asked.
> "I will make him a salamander bed to sleep in. I will cover him with leaves that are fresh and green, and bring moss that looks like little stars to be a pillow for his head."

The Day Jimmy's Boa Ate the Wash
by Trinka Hakes Noble, 1980, Dial Books for Young Readers, NY

> "Well, what finally stopped it?"
> "Well, we heard the farmer's wife screaming."
> "Why was she screaming?"
> "We never found out because Mrs. Stanley made us get on the bus, and we sort of left in a hurry without the boa constrictor."

WRITING CONNECTION — ...and Telling Them How to Say Them

As the students did for "Putting Words in Their Mouths" in the last lesson, have them choose comic strips and rewrite the stories as dialogue. Challenge students to find precise and vivid verbs for their tags.

WRITING CONNECTION — Tag Less, Talk More

Have students write stories without dialogue tags. Remind them to consider the difficulties this might pose for readers, and ask them in advance if they think these stories will be difficult to write.

WRITERS' WALL — Writers' Wall

Let students collect and post effective tags they write or find in their readings. You might want to list substitutes for *said: replied, objected, hollered, gasped, sighed, denied, whined,* and so on.

Ellipsis

Student Objective

To understand the function of the ellipsis.

Background

Young writers are not commonly taught the ellipsis, but because it occurs fairly often in children's books, and students will both need to "read" it and want to imitate the use of it, the ellipsis is worth teaching.

An *ellipsis* is three periods (...), sometimes four, and its purpose can be difficult to pin down. It can signal a pause or a trailing off in speech or narration. It can also signal that there's more to come, or something coming... And it can stand in for text missing from a quotation (in fact, *ellipsis* also means the omission of part of a sentence itself), though your students probably won't use the ellipsis as a stand-in until later in their academic careers.

She saw the figure...white and shimmering.

(slow down, more to come; imagine that the subject is having some difficulty seeing the "figure," maybe because of fog)

Sue said, "I can't..." and then sat down.

(Sue trails off into woolgathering, perhaps sullen...)

Lesson

The Elusive Ellipsis

Show students the ellipsis, discuss its uses, and share examples of it from books they know. Talk about how authors use the ellipsis to influence the way we read. In *Barn Dance!* (see below), for example, the character leaves the whirl of a square dance and settles down at home, still feeling the pleasure:

> He tiptoed through the kitchen...an' tiptoed up the stairs...
>
> As quiet as a feather...on a breath of air...

In *If at First You Do Not See* (see below), an ellipsis indicates that the caterpillar pauses to admire what it sees and come to a decision about it:

> "Look at that lovely clump of grass...I think I'll taste it," said the caterpillar.

Wrap-up

Discuss situations for stories that might be well served by ellipses. This discussion can also be a prewriting activity for suspense or detective stories, since the ellipsis can hold action back, back...SURPRISE!

Extension Activities

The Purpose of the Ellipsis Is...

Give small groups of students books that rely on ellipses (see Literature Connection, below). Groups discuss their book's intention (its subject and mood) and record their conclusions about the purpose of the ellipses. When groups are ready, hold a discussion about their results. Lead students to come up with general guidelines for using ellipses that can be posted on the Writers' Wall.

And...It's...Oh, No!

Pass out cards which describe suspenseful, dangerous, tricky, or frightening situations. Students then each write a sentence or two about a situation, using ellipses.

Haunted House
"What's that…noise?"
She crawled…she stumbled…she finally got to the door.

A Football Game
"Mmm…a hot dog tastes better at a game," said Bob.
There's the snap…the kick…it's wobbling…wobbling…through the uprights! It's good!

Literature Connection

Of course, a variety of children's books contain ellipses. Below are just a few:

If at First You Do Not See
by Ruth Brown, 1982, Henry Holt and Company, NY

The reader turns this book around and around, and the pictures keep changing. The quotation below accompanies a mushroom changing into two witches:

Oh, look! A delicious mushroom!
That definitely looks good enough to eat.
But I'll just have a look to make sure it's safe.
Eeeek! It's a good thing I did…
I don't like the looks of those two—

Barn Dance!
By Bill Martin Jr. and John Archambault, 1986, The Trumpet Club, NY

The ol' dog stretched 'n blinked a sleepy eye
Just a blink too late to see the skinny kid slip by…

Rechenka's Eggs
by Patricia Palacco, 1988, Scholastic Inc., NY

"Look at them," the elders said. "They almost glow…as if the paint is part of the shell itself."

The judges picked Babushka's eggs as the most beautiful! Babushka was so happy. She beamed as she looked at the First Prize…a feather-bed quilt!

And So They Build
by Bert Kitchen, 1993, Candlewick Press, Cambridge, MA

A male satin bowerbird is looking for a mate and so he builds…
Satin bowerbirds live in the rainforests of eastern Australia…

My Mama Says There Aren't Any Zombies, Ghosts, Vampires, Creatures, Demons, Monsters, Fiends, Goblins, or Things
by Judith Viorst, 1973, The Trumpet Club, NY

But yesterday my mama said I couldn't have some cream cheese on my sandwich, because, she said, there wasn't any more.

And then I found the cream cheese under the lettuce in back of the Jello. So…sometimes even mamas make mistakes.

Model Ellipsis

With *And So They Build* (above) as a model for using ellipses, ask, *What's unique about what ellipses do in this book? What's the effect of ending a factual statement with punctuation that trails off, telling the reader, "There's more here…"* Discuss the effect with the class, and then challenge them to write their own similar pieces. These can be invented stories or research pieces, as you choose.

Model Ellipsis II

Have students choose an animal and then write about its adventures according to the following model. Explain that the object is to create suspenseful situations or predicaments for the animal that can be indicated with ellipses.

The curious cat left home.
The cat sees a dog…
Run cat run.
She runs down an alley and then sees another cat…
Run cat run.

She hides under a tree and meets a snake…
Run cat run.

Writers' Wall

Post examples of sentences with ellipses as references before students work on the lesson's activities. Later, exhibit student work for "And…It's…Oh, No!"

Dash

Student Objective

To understand the two functions of the dash—introducing an explanation or interrupting.

Background

A dash can signal a sudden interruption of thought (*Barnaby's coat—the coat Allison had lent him—was caught in the door*) or of speech (*No, Allison gave me—*). A dash can also mean *that is* (or *namely, in other words, i.e.*, and so on): *Agatha's homework weighed on her—books for every class stuffed her backpack so that she groaned picking it up.*

Lesson

Writing With Dash

Copy O'Neill's "Dash" and ask for volunteers to read it aloud. After two readings, ask students if they can figure out what the dash is used for. Model their explanations of how to use the dash, explaining in turn whether they got it right. Then post a few clear examples and explain the proper use of the dash.

DASH

Dash is a sign that writers make
Whenever their thoughts switch or break.

Wrap-up

Let students try to write sentences that use dashes correctly. First call out, *Use the dash as an interrupter*, and give the class some time to work out a complete sentence. Share and discuss the results. Then call out, *Use the dash to introduce an explanation*, as if it meant *that is*. Again, discuss the results.

Extension Activities

A Dash of Noel Coward

Tell students that they are going to dramatize the dash by performing interrupted telephone conversations. Before students pair up to create their own quick "interruption plays," choose three actors for the sketch below as a demonstration. One actor plays Virgil, the caller; one actor plays the illustrious part of the Dash, miming the noble punctuation's service as interrupter; the third actor will play the part of Clarice after the class, as a group, has written the part. (Virgil and the Dash may need to run through their roles once before curtain.) For the first performance, Virgil and Dash act out this sample conversation.

Virgil: Hello. It's Virgil. Is—
         Yes, I did want to talk to—
         Ah, Clarice. How are—
         Really! I—
         I'd love to—
         Eight o'clock—
         Ta ta.

On the second performance, the Dash signals a pause, at which point the class provides Clarice's half of the conversation; the student chosen to be Clarice records the dialogue. When the part of Clarice is written, the three actors perform the play a third and final time, to a standing ovation!

With that success fresh in mind, pairs write their own interruption plays, leaving out—but never forgetting!—the part of the Dash. As a mnemonic aid for the performers, so they tie the interruptions directly to punctuation, you can have them flash a dash card whenever they interrupt.

As separate performances, or built into single plays, you can also have students dramatize the dash as interrupting thought. Use the sketch below as a model, and then let students write their own plays. You may even want to perform the plays for parents or other classes.

Dithers: Hello. It's Dithers. That you, Klemp?

Klemp: I should say it is.

Dithers: Well, then, Klemp—if it really is you—
          let's go on a camping trip, on Saturday!

Klemp: It's November, Dith-

Dithers: Yes, Klemp, but Saturday—if you didn't
          know—is my birthday!

Klemp: My dear Dithers—and I'm sorry to say

I didn't know—well of course we're going camping. I'll bring the pelican!

Late-Breaking Ideas

Arrange students in groups and pass out interrupting-idea cards, 12 per group. Students must think of situations in which the scripted changes in thought might occur. They then write sentences that include the interruptions or changes in thought. Some possible interrupters are:

—if you didn't know—
—not even a mouse—
—but still warm—
—about 20 minutes away—
—oh no!—
—not that she cared—

And the last example might produce: *Everyone had already left for the football game—not that she even wanted to go.*

Literature Connection

The books below present dashes at their best:

Brave Irene
by William Steig, 1986, Farrar, Straus, & Giroux, NY

Then—oh, woe!—the box was wrenched from her mittened grasp and sent bumbling along in the snow.

Up North in Winter
by Deborah Hartley, 1986, Puffin Unicorn Books, NY

In the distance, he could see the lights of his own town–about a three-hour walk away.

The Magic Fan
by Keith Baker, 1989, Harcourt Brace & Company, NY

"A bridge—it will arch from end to end over the village."

"First the boat, then the kite, and now the

bridge—we do not need these things. Why has Yoshi built them?"

Drama Into Print

Invite students to draw cartoons—complete with balloons or captions and, of course, appropriate dashes—of the telephone plays they wrote for "A Dash of Noel Coward."

Unfortunately With Dash

Challenge students to write "Fortunately/Unfortunately" stories that feature changes of thought in each sen-tence. (Introduce this activity with *Fortunately* by Remy Charlip [The Trumpet Club, 1964]).

Fortunately, Brice—the world traveler—started on his trip through the desert. Unfortunately, a sandstorm—about twenty minutes into the trip—halted his progress. Fortunately, a camel—not the prettiest of animals—came lumbering along…

Writers' Wall

Post defining examples of proper dash use at the beginning of the unit; the example plays from "A Dash of Noel Coward" would be useful. Later, exhibit the students' successful plays, cartoons, and sentences.

Forms and Functions of SENTENCES

Now that your students have learned about, talked about, and experimented with the components of grammar, it's time for them integrate their knowledge and apply it to building sentences. Of course, writers don't commonly make their sentences by thinking, *Okay, first I need a noun, then I'll tack on an adjective*. The operation is a back and forth between knowing what to write and searching for what words will come next. But students do need to learn how sentences hold together, and how they can be taken apart, so they can manipulate sentences until they say what they mean them to say, as precisely as possible. In other words, sentences themselves are components and can be added to, shortened, and rearranged as needed in order to fit the larger mechanism that is the piece of writing.

Two-Partedness

Student Objective

To understand that the simplest sentence must have a subject and predicate.

Background

While it's accepted that a sentence is a *complete thought, expressed by a subject and a predicate*, and while students can be made to memorize such a definition, doing only that will help only a very few of them to actually build their own correct sentences. Students certainly do need to know what subjects and predicates are so that everyone can talk together about writing. But the best way to *learn* sentence structure for the largest portion of your students, and the most exciting and satisfying way for *all* students, is to play at building and taking apart the types of sentences they come across in their readings. And, of course, reading, reading, reading is crucial to learning to use language.

Lesson

Sentences Under Construction

Post the first stanza of O'Neill's "A Sentence" and ask volunteers to read it aloud twice. Then discuss the definition of sentence, asking, *What does complete thought mean? What's the complete thought expressed in the example sentence in the poem? Can you figure out, based on what we've learned so far, what the subject of the sentence is, and what the predicate is? Based on that example, can you define* subject *and* predicate? Lead students to articulate that the basic sentence has two parts: the subject is the part of the sentence the rest of the sentence is speaking about, and the predicate is the part that speaks about the subject.

A SENTENCE

A sentence is a group of words
expressing a complete thought.
It needs a subject and a predicate:
The kidnapper was caught.

Wrap-up

Invite students to come to the chalkboard and write subjects, then have others come up and write predicates, encouraging students to have fun making up ridiculous sentences about amusing characters. Have them start writing the simplest kinds of simple sentences (a simple sentence is one independent clause)—*Mrs. Dawes screamed.* Then let them write increasingly involved simple sentences—*Spookily thin and crabby Mrs. Dawes screamed herself hoarse.*

Extension Activities

Domino Sentence Scramble

In groups of four, students write 20 simple sentences on strips and then cut the strips into subject- and predicate-dominoes. Students shuffle the dominoes and then each takes four and lays them out upside down in a line. The game begins with one of the remaining four dominoes placed face up in the center of the table. Players take turns turning over their first strips, on the left, and trying to add them to the face-up dominoes to complete sentences.

If players cannot make proper sentences, they move their dominoes to the end of their rows and try to use them again later. Then the next player goes. If no one can add to the center domino or dominoes, then one of the remaining dominoes must be added to the center. The first player to use all four dominoes wins.

Give students patterns to follow for writing their sentences, such as *single subject + is + -ing form of a verb (The teacher is singing)*, or *singular subject + past tense (The explorer traveled)*, or *non-living plural things + present tense (Clocks tick)*, and so on. Of course, the scrambled sentences will work technically, but they'll be bizarre and entertaining, too *(The teacher is camping; Clocks eat)*.

Sentence Rodeo

In an adaptation of the game "Lasso," invented by Eric Solomon, pairs or trios of students write random subjects and predicates in three columns on a page. They then take turns "lassoing" sentences by looping lines around subjects (or subject phrases) and predicates (or predicate phrases). However, players may not circle a phrase already lassoed and cannot intersect another lasso. In the example below, a player could not lasso *Two girls* and *sang opera* but could lasso *Two cows* and *had a birthday party*.

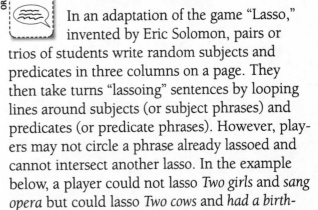

The two sisters	ate 6 donuts	Jack and Jill
tried to sleep	sang opera	two cows
Six fat geese	played hockey	two girls
Seven hungry snakes	read mysteries	had a birthday party
shopped	tried to sleep	a hundred ants

Literature Connection

Below are alphabet books that feature rich, vivid diction in simple sentences:

African Animals ABC
by Philippa-Alys Browne, 1995, Sierra Club Books for Children, San Francisco, CA

> Antbear naps.
> Bushbaby blinks.
> Crocodile snaps.

The Cowboy ABC
by Chris Demarest, 1999, A DK Ink Book, NY

> A is for Appaloosa, a trusty steed.
> B is for Buckaroo, who rides at top speed.
> C is the Cattle, that follow the trail.
> D is the Dog, wagging his tail.

The A to Z Beastly Jamboree
by Robert Bender, 1996, Lodestar Books, NY

> Ants anchor Aa
> Bats boil Bb
> Cows carry Cc

The next book, also an abecedary, presents alliterative sentences as well as phrases that students can combine to make sentences:

Animalia
by Graham Base, 1986, Harry N. Abrams, Inc., NY

> An Armoured Armadillo Avoiding An Angry Alligator.

The next two books include grammatically incomplete sentences that nonetheless work in the stories. Explain that the authors decided to write such sentences, and discuss why they might have done so. Ask students if they find the writing successful.

The Glorious Flight Across the Channel With Louis Bleriot, July 25, 1909
by Alice and Martin Provensen, 1987, Puffin Books, NY

> "CRUMP!" goes the car. Into the cart of Alphonse Juvet.

My Mama Says There Aren't Any Zombies, Ghosts, Vampires, Creatures, Demons, Monsters, Fiends,

Goblins, or Things
by Judith Viorst, 1973, The Trumpet Club, NY

> And that's how there get to be scrambled eggs all over my shoes. And that lady.

Soundly Sequential Sentences

Challenge students to write their own alliterative sentences, like *Slow snakes slither silently*. Students can write their own alliterative ABC's and even illustrate them and give them to younger students. When their writing is finished, ask each student to share a favorite subject and a favorite predicate.

The ABC's of the Sentence

Have students write sentences in which words run in alphabetical order, like *All boats cruise dangerously each Friday*.

Riddle Maps

Invite students to write riddle poems describing geographical locations. Require that each line be a complete two-part sentence.

> **Where Am I?**
> Sand is blowing.
> Dunes are forming.   (Desert)
> Mirages shimmer.
> Oasis gives life.

Writers' Wall

Show students how to diagram their simple sentences and exhibit some on the Wall as a reference. Write simple subjects at the left, simple predicates at the right, and divide them with a slash. Write articles, adjectives, adverbs, objects of the predicate, and prepositional phrases on slanting lines underneath the word they modify, as below.

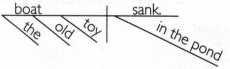

Expanding Sentences

Student Objective

To understand how to expand a sentence by adding detail.

Background

Complicated sentences are not necessarily more desirable than simple sentences, but writers certainly need to know how and when to build them. To attain the flexibility that lets a writer swing back and forth between the simple and the complicated, students need to practice expanding simple sentences by adding detail. At the same time, they get to hear that individual sentences have rhythm, and sentences link together to make a larger rhythm. So, playing with expanding sentences lets student writers investigate and develop their own writing styles.

Lesson

The Ancient Building Blocks of Sentences

Copy the "building-block" pyramid (below) on the chalkboard and discuss how including significant detail in sentences lets writers convey important meaning to readers. Lead students through the stages of the pyramid, explaining that each line is a sentence (the top line is an imperative, which has an *implied* subject). Then ask, *If I were writing a report or story about elephants, why might I use the longest sentence instead of the others?* Lead students to articulate that the longest sentence gives the reader specific information about which elephants are stomping and why they are doing so (the bulls stomp *menacingly*, perhaps to ward off danger).

Stomp!
Elephants stomp.
Angry elephants stomp.
Angry bull elephants stomp.
Angry bull elephants stomp menacingly.

Wrap-up

Run through constructing a model pyramid with students. Call on volunteers to provide words; if you need to start them off, try imperatives for things students like to do (*play, bicycle, chew, read,* and so on). Then hand student-pairs sheets with outlined pyramids of 15 building blocks (a block for each word), like the elephant one. The pairs fill in the pyramids top to bottom by starting with an imperative and adding a single word at each stage. Share the results.

Extension Activities

ORAL LANGUAGE

Modern Building Tiles

Dramatize building sentences stone by stone, or tile by tile, by providing each student with large cards on which they will write words they want to contribute to the group sentence. Begin by having two students stand at the front of the room, each holding a word card and forming a kernel sentence, such as *Students learn.* Then a third student writes a word that will expand the kernel sentence and joins the two at the front in the appropriate position: *All students learn.* Continue in this way, adding students and words one at a time until students cannot expand the sentence, or it's just time to move on, and then start a new one.

Columns of Words

Have groups of students build sentences in short columns (maybe four or five words tall) by each contributing one word. If a sentence is completed, the next student simply starts a new one. As students get used to the process, challenge them to write sentences that wrap columns (a sentence not finished at the bottom of one column can start the next column). The column form highlights the word-by-word construction of sentences.

Literature Connection

Animalia
by Graeme Base, 1986, Harry N. Abrams, Inc., NY

Although not all the passages are sentences, students can still talk about how simple subjects and predicates are expanded with rich detail.

> …richly robed rhinoceroses riding in rickety red rickshaws…
> …six slithering snakes sliding silently southward…

A Snake is Totally Tail
by Judi Barrett, 1983, Macmillan Publishing Company, NY

Here, simple sentences are expanded with adverbs. Invite students to add alliterative adjectives to further expand the sentences.

> *A seal is seemingly slippery* might become
> *A shimmering seal is seemingly slippery.*

Share books which present detailed simple sentences and also compound and complex sentences. Challenge students to find kernel sentences (the simple subject and simple predicate) and then discuss how the author expanded the sentence. One good book for this exercise is:

Rumpelstiltskin
by Paul O. Zelinsky, 1986, Dutton Children's Books, NY

1) Shortly after sunrise the king returned.
2) And in a fury he jumped on his cooking spoon and flew out the window.

The kernel sentences are: 1) *The king returned*; 2) *He jumped and flew.*

Pass-Around Stories

A fun story-writing version of "Columns of Words" is to pass several pages around the class at once. On each page students contribute single words that make sense following what was contributed before, writing different group stories *word by word*! The resulting stories are often hysterically funny and will certainly provide fodder for discussing how sentences are built.

Windows Onto Sentences

Invite students to make their own flap-page stories by expanding single sentences (such as *Find the buried treasure*) so that they address any or all of the following questions: what, where, when, who, how, and why. Students first write their sentences, then expand them to suit the questions that will label the flaps, as seen below.

Find the buried treasure

(*Where*) on the beach; (*When*) when the moon is full; (*How*) by counting five paces from the palm tree; (*Why*) because everyone wants a trunkful of coconuts.

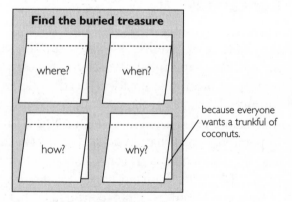

Writers' Wall

Students can diagram the longest sentences from their pyramids and post them on the Wall.

Substitutions

Student Objective

To understand how and why to substitute one word for another.

Background

Crafting a precise and vivid sentence requires sifting through one's internal word bank for just the right one or revising an existing sentence by substituting a more effective word for a stale one. Practicing substituting words, then, lets students see the inner workings of sentences from another angle and also gives them a basic and concrete experience of revising.

Lesson

Substitute Teaching

Discuss the possibility of substituting words, explaining that as long as a new word is the same part of speech as one already in a sentence, that new word can be substituted for the old one. Remind students of any "mad libs" activities they've done (such as "Putting Them All Together," page 32); point out that "mad libs" involve filling in blanks with any word that is the appropriate part of speech. (You might want to model an example or show them a familiar "mad lib.") Explain that often writers will want to replace words in first drafts with other words that more precisely say what they mean. So instead of substituting any word that's the right part of speech, they will be learning to substitute words that mean almost the same thing as the old word but fit the meaning and the tone more precisely.

Write the following sentence on the chalkboard, underlining as in the example:

The <u>man</u> <u>walked</u> to the <u>store</u>.

man	walked	store
mailman	ambled	post office
adult	strode	office
boy	shuffled	class

Ask students to identify the underlined parts of speech. Discuss the meaning and tone of the original sentence, then substitute words and discuss the differences. Substitute *shuffled* for *walked*, for instance, and ask, *What kind of person do you see shuffling to the store? Why might a man shuffle instead of walk to the store?* (Be aware that most students will comprehend the differences in tone and meaning more readily than they will be able to discuss the abstract rule of substituting same parts of speech.)

Extension Activities

Skipping Joyously Word to Word

Divide the class into groups of three to four and pass out copies (one per group) of a five-word sentence, underlined as above, such as *The big dinosaur roamed thunderously.* The groups then find four substitutes for each word of the sentence except the noun. One group, for instance, might write, A *huge* dinosaur *wandered aimlessly*; *One pet* dinosaur *skipped joyously*; *Their huge* dinosaur *trudged heavily*, and so on. Groups should record their sentences in neat rows so that they can read them not only straight across, but jumping from line to line as well, generating even more variations.

Substitute Word Scramble

Write another five-word sentence on cards, one word per card, and have students write substitute words on their own cards. (Assign students parts of speech or let each come up with a substitute for every word but the noun.) Have five volunteers hold the starting-sentence cards in order at the front of the room, and then ask, for instance, *Who has a substitution for the verb?* Students raise their hands if they want to substitute their verb for the starting one, and students holding the starting words call on others to replace them. Continue until everyone has had a chance to be part of the sentence or all the variations are exhausted.

Literature Connection

Investigate the diction of favorite or current authors, explaining that authors decide to use the words they use. Ask students, *What is the effect of using this word? What other words could work here, and what does this one do that no other one could do?* (Note: It is important to lead students to discuss the *effects* of diction as opposed to the author's *rationale* for using a given word, since we cannot know what the author had in mind.)

Once Upon A Golden Apple
by Jean Little and Maggie De Vries, 1991, Puffin Books, NY

Black and White
by David Macauley, 1990, Houghton Mifflin Company, Boston

Choose-Your-Own-Story Mural

Invite students to work together to create a mural story that lets readers slot in a variety of characters and events. First, help students write a template story: Ask the class or individuals to write single sentences that present the setting, the characters, the beginning, a problem or critical event, the resolution of the problem or result of the event, and the ending. Write these sentences on a poster-sized page (or several large sheets connected), separated by a fair amount of space, as if they were paragraph headings, leaving room for words to come. Post them on a bulletin board or the Writers' Wall. Then, under every story sentence, students compile lists of words and phrases to substitute for the various parts of that sentence. Readers can read the original story straight through or substitute characters, situations, and details, as they choose. (You might notice that strict substitutions can be difficult to figure out and give the story a stilted, or inappropriately archaic, tone. If you like, and to make it a little easier for students, let them rearrange the order of parts of speech if they're having trouble.)

Once upon a time	there lived	a giant	in a	cold castle.
One cold and rainy night	up walked	a lonely child	to a	rickety old mansion.
A long time ago	there slept	a princess	in an	impenetrable fortress

Slotted Sentence Flip Books

Invite students to write and publish their own slotted sentence flip books. Students make books by stapling several strips of paper

74

(about 3x8 inches) together along their top edges, lengthwise. They then divide the strips into three equal columns and cut them from the bottom, leaving an adequate margin at the top to hold the book together; tell them to leave the last page of the book intact. Next, students write a sentence and divide it into three parts (subject, verb, complement). They write each part in a column on the last page of the flip book. Then, on each of the strips above the original sentence, students write substitute words and phrases that would work as subject, verb, and complement, respectively.

Writers' Wall

Exhibit the sentence and alternate words from the lesson as a reference. Later, show off the "Choose-Your-Own-Story Mural."

Combining Sentences

Student Objective

To understand how simple sentences can be combined into more complicated sentences.

Background

In order to grow as writers—and that means to leave behind monotonous writing and begin sounding authoritative—students need to practice combining simple sentences into longer, detailed ones.

Lesson

Frogs Into Princes

Remind students of their goal of writing precisely and persuasively, and explain that, toward this end, they will work on combining simple sentences into more complicated ones. While they did learn one way to combine sentences when they worked on linking two independent clauses by a conjunction and a comma, this lesson will focus on combining ideas from two or more sentences into one richly detailed simple sentence.

Write two sentences on the chalkboard with which to model sentence combining, such as *I want my bike,* and *My bike is at the repair shop.* Then invite a student to the chalkboard to combine them: *I want my bike that is at the repair shop,* or *I want my bike from the repair shop.* Next, present three sentences to be combined into one, such as *I like frogs, Frogs are green,* and *Frogs can hop.* Then invite a second student to the chalkboard to try combining them: *I like green frogs that can hop.*

Some students, of course, may not recognize the most direct ways to combine sentences and may come up with intricate, confusing solutions, such as *Frogs that are green and can hop I like,* or even *Green frogs I like that can hop.* Suggest to everyone that they start with the subject of the sentence and work from there, reminding them that the subject is the one who is doing the action of the sentence.

Extension Activities

Interlocking Combinations

Divide students into groups of three or four and have one student in each group write a simple sentence that has a subject, verb, and object: *Jill has a ball* (students can add articles as needed). The second student must then revise the sentence, substituting a different object for the original and a different verb, if necessary: *Jill is a fifth grader*. The third student uses the object from the first sentence as a subject and supplies a new object (and verb, if necessary): *The ball is red*. Finally, the fourth student substitutes a new object or adjective, depending on what the verb has changed to: *The ball is striped*. This is complicated to explain, but once it's modeled, students should be able, and will be excited, to try it. The result is a monotonous series of sentences that students must then combine into one or two more complicated sentences: *The red, striped ball belongs to Jill, a fifth grader,* or *A fifth grader, Jill, has a red, striped ball.*

Team Combo

Arrange students in combination teams, and challenge each team to come up with four sentences that they must rewrite as a single sentence four different ways. The original four sentences must be between three and five words and deal with the same subject. Teams receive one point for each combined sentence; all the information of the original four sentences must be included in each new sentence. Set a time limit that's reasonable for your class's abilities.

> The cows ambled in the meadow.
> The cows eat the clover.
> They chew their cud.
> They make milk.

1) The cows amble and eat the clover in the meadow, chew their cud, and make milk.

2) Chewing their cud and making milk, the cows amble and eat the clover in the meadow.

3) In the meadow, cows eat the clover and chew their cud as they amble in the meadow making milk.

4) The cows make milk by eating the clover and chewing their cud while ambling in the meadow.

Literature Connection

Any good picture book abounds in compact sentences that students can "uncombine," rewriting them as separate simple sentences. Challenge students to uncombine sentences. Alternatively, uncombine published sentences for your students, then have them recombine them and check their results against the original. Here's an example of the original sentence and an uncombined version from *Brave Irene* by William Steig:

> She coaxed her mother into bed, covered her with two quilts, and added a blanket for her feet.
> She coaxed her mother into bed.
> She covered her with two quilts.
> She added a blanket for her feet.

The Haiku Packs It In

Let students choose illustrations to describe in four simple sentences. They then combine the four into a haiku of one or two detailed sentences. In English, the basic haiku form is three lines of five, seven, and five syllables, respectively.

Before:
> The wild flowers are yellow.
> The flowers blow in the breeze.
> There is a field of wild flowers.
> A woman walks through the field.

After:
> Caressed by breeze are
> the woman who walks there and
> the yellow flowers.

Writers' Wall

Post simple and combined sentences from the lesson as a reference, then exhibit student haikus at the end of the unit. You might want to hold a poetry reading for the class, for another class, or for the parents.

Varying Sentence Length

Student Objective

To understand the need to vary sentence length in order to maintain reader interest.

Background

Sentence variety is, of course, essential to good writing, and even young writers cannot only recognize this but apply that recognition to their own work. While there are no rules (at least no accurate ones) about how to establish a compelling rhythm–since rhythm in language depends not only on relative length of sentences but on types of beginnings and endings, syllables and sounds, and so on–playing with sentence length will help student writers figure out how to excite and soothe, command and coddle, persuade and enchant their readers.

Lesson

I Got Rhythm (and Tone)

Discuss the writer's need for and the reader's pleasure in varying sentence length. Ask, *Based on the work with sentences we've done so far, do you agree that it's important to use different kinds of sentences when you write? Why or why not? What do you like an author to do with sentences? Does it depend on what the subject is?* Then read aloud to the class from one of the books mentioned in this section's Literature Connection, alerting them to the variety of sentence lengths they will hear. Ask them to try to hear the rhythm of the story and, if you can, try to dramatize the rhythm when you read.

Wrap-up

In advance, invite students to bring in their favorite stories so they can read them aloud. For homework the night before, you might ask them to read the story at home (maybe aloud to their parents), noting the kinds of sentences and the rhythm. Ask, *Can you describe the rhythm of the story? Does it change with the events or the feelings?* Invite students to read their favorite stories to the class-you might want to schedule readings over several days-and remind them to try to read with an ear for the rhythm.

Extension Activities

ORAL LANGUAGE

Sentence Building Tic-Tac-Toe

Challenge students to play "sentence

tic-tac-toe" in pairs or teams. In order to win spaces, players must first construct sentences according to the directions inside them. When they win squares, they place card stock x's and o's inside. (You will have to build the boards and the X's and O's.) Square directions and successful answers might run as follows:

1-word imperative	Listen!
3-word sentence	You eat cheese.
8-word sentence	Alex left the building, but Martha waited inside.
a sentence with *because*	I rocked the test because I studied.
a sentence with *if*	If I had studied, I would have rocked the test.
2 commas in the sentence	Julius, who loves oranges, wouldn't eat the grapefruit.

Topic Sentence Building by Numbers

ORAL LANGUAGE

Make up two sets of cards, one of numbers ranging from three to eight, the other of topics from some area of the class curriculum. Divide students into groups of four to six; one person draws the group's topic and each person draws a number. Each student must create, on the spot and orally, a sentence about the topic using exactly the number of words indicated on the drawn card. Thus each group together writes a short-short story or expository paragraph.

> Topic: The Trip to the Zoo
>
> 5: It was a rainy day.
> 3: We were mad!
> 6: We were going to the zoo.
> 7: We trudged through mud to the bus.
> 4: The bus got stuck.
> 8: We trudged back through mud to our classroom.

Literature Connection

LITERATURE CONNECTION

Here are a few books that feature a variety of sentence lengths:

Owl Moon
by Jane Yolen, 1987, Scholastic Inc., NY

Condor's Egg
by Jonathan London, 1994, Chronicle Books, San Francisco

Comet's Nine Lives
by Jan Brett, 1996, Scholastic Inc., NY

Akiak: A Tale From the Iditarod
by Robert J. Blake, 1997, Scholastic Inc., NY

Expository Exploring

WRITING CONNECTION

Using *Condor's Egg* as a model, have students write a one-page factually based story. You might have them pick topics from the curriculum or their own interests. When they have finished a rough draft, have them assess the degree to which they varied sentence length (some students may even benefit from actually counting words) and, if necessary, revise their pieces by combining sentences.

Portrait Poems

WRITING CONNECTION

As a class, brainstorm sentence requirements like those used in "Sentence Building Tic-Tac-Toe." Students then meet the requirements for a minimum of five sentences that they will use in "Portrait Poems." (They might write about people in their lives or people they've read about.) The poems begin with a one- or two-word name. The second line should be a two- or three-word description of the subject. The next lines are the sentences written in advance; they can appear in any order that suits the poet. The last two lines are a reprise of lines two and then one. Sentence requirements might include: *a short descriptive sentence of five or six words; a sentence with a color; a sentence with because; a long sentence of 14 or 15 words; a question; a sentence with one adjective and one adverb; a sentence with the word wish; and so on.*

Mom,
My best friend.
The color yellow reminds me of her
    because she's always upbeat and happy.
What do I wish for her?
I wish her a long life.

My best friend,
Mom.

Writers' Wall
Exhibit the Portrait Poems.

Audience and Purpose

Student Objective

To be aware that there are many kinds of writing, and that these address specific audiences.

Background

As discussed at the beginning of the last chapter, writing assumes an *audience*, and because there are many different audiences, there are many kinds of writing. Experimenting with a variety of forms lets student writers apply their knowledge of grammar and vocabulary, of course, and it also lets them investigate *voice*—the *manner* in which writing addresses its audience. As students try their pens at different kinds of writing, they have to ask themselves, *Why am I writing this? What am I trying to accomplish? And who am I trying to persuade, enchant, inform?* Keeping the audience in mind enables the writer to find the voice that will best accomplish the purpose of the piece of writing. And, to reiterate from a slightly different angle, because there are many purposes for writing, there are many kinds of writing:

persuasive writing tries to get someone to agree with a point of view

expressive writing makes feelings known

narrative writing tells a story, whether factual or invented

descriptive writing paints a word-picture

expository writing explains a topic

poetry can do any and all of the above, often with exquisite attention to language itself

Lesson

Audience Appeal

Assign students the task of bringing in examples of a variety of writing, such as letters, advertisements, bills, articles, greeting cards, and solicitations, as well as stories and poems. On the chalkboard, record the students' contributions under the appropriate categories, as described above. While doing this, explain the categories by discussing the purposes and target audiences of the pieces of writing. Ask, about advertisements, for instance, *Does this interest you? Who do you think would care about this ad? Now remember, somebody wrote this ad in order to sell the product, so who do you think they are targeting?* About bills you might ask, *Can you describe the*

language of this bill? Why does the company speak this way to its customers? What do you think they want you to think and feel about the company?

Wrap-up

Explain that we usually think about our audience when we speak or write, even if we do so unconsciously. For an object lesson in addressing audiences, have students choose two people to write letters to: one person should be someone they are comfortable chatting with; the other should be someone they would only speak to politely. To demonstrate their task, say, *Imagine that you just saw a great movie. It had a lot of jokes that cracked you up. You're telling your friend about it: how do you describe it, what kinds of words do you use? Now imagine you're telling the principal: do you describe the same movie differently, using different kinds of words?* When students have finished their letters, discuss the results.

Extension Activities

Generating Genres

Have students brainstorm a list of topics on a theme, from the curriculum or of general interest, and then record the topics on cards. Arrange the class in small groups and distribute the cards. Students must think of three different kinds of writing they could use to address the topics they have drawn. For example, if a student chooses *baseball* as a topic, possible kinds of writing might be *contract, statistics sheet, advertisement in which a player appears, article,* or *history.*

Breaking the Code

Divide the class into groups of four or five, and give each group a broad sampling of books and magazines (textbooks,

baby books, sports magazines, newspapers, and so on). The groups figure out and record the age group that is each sample's intended audience. When the groups are finished, discuss their results and how they came to their conclusions. What did they go by: size of type, illustrations, diction? If relevant for particular kinds of writing, such as ads, ask, *Are there any other audiences this piece is geared for?*

Literature Connection

The books below each present several kinds of writing:

The High Rise Glorious Skittle Skat Roarious Sky Pie Angel Food Cake
by Nancy Willard, 1990, Harcourt Brace & Company, NY
(includes: recipes, poetry, journal writing, and a saying)

Three Days on a River in a Red Canoe
by Vera B. Williams, 1981, Mulberry Books, NY
(includes: maps, captions, recipes, and directions)

Seabird
by Holling Clancy, 1948, The Trumpet Club, NY
(includes: expository writing, newspaper clippings, maps, sketches, drawings, and captions)

"George Gershwin"
by Mike Venezia in *Getting to Know the World's Greatest Composers,* 1994, Children's Press, Chicago
(includes: cartoons, photos, drawings, posters, and paintings with captions)

Any Way You Choose

Let students select topics they would like to write about. Then have them list ten different forms of writing they could use to address the topic, and five different audiences they could write for. They then choose a final form and a final audience and write about their topic. Depending on time of year, student, mood of class, and so on, you might encourage students to choose forms that would conventionally be used to address their topics (an expository essay to talk about Churchill) or to choose forms that would never be used to address their topics (an advertising jingle about Churchill).

Mixed but not Muddled

Challenge students to write one piece about a chosen topic that incorporates two (or more, if they like) forms of writing, such as an expository piece that includes an invented newspaper clipping, or a poem that interrupts itself to present a short play.

Writers' Wall

Let students sort and post by category the pieces of writing brought in for the lesson.

Leads

Student Objective

To understand that leads greatly influence reader interest.

Background

A *lead* is the first sentence or group of sentences of a piece, and it is the lead's job to hook readers, making them want to read more. Leads may introduce the subject or situation but do so in a provocative way, tempting readers with only partial information, attracting them in emotionally charged language, startling them with a seemingly impossible event, and so on. As with creating a rhythm, there are no set rules for writing successful leads, but, as Donald Murray explains in *Shoptalk: Learning to Write With Writers*, it is not time wasted to put effort into writing first lines. In addition to the value leads have as hooks, crafting strong leads is like building a solid foundation that is also the blueprint for the rest of the structure, ". . . because the writing has found its voice, its aim, its destination before the writer has written a paragraph" (Murray, 119).

Drafting leads and tinkering with them until they're up and running lets students see from the inside that writing well is a process. And again, while there are no definite rules about what makes good leads any more than what makes compelling rhythm, student writers will develop skills and knowledge about their own styles by practicing specific kinds of leads (such as beginning with action, dialogue, description, a question, or any combination of writing elements).

Lesson

Lead Off With the Right Hook

Present a variety of book covers and explain that publishers make book covers to attract potential readers. So the illustration (painting, photograph, and so on) on the cover is meant to present a tantalizing preview of what's in store for someone who reads the book. (Of course, covers often distort a book's actual story or content.) Explain that the book's lead has to pick up where the cover left off: the lead has to persuade readers to keep on reading.

Read a successful lead from one of the books and discuss why it is successful. Guide students to articulate the means used to hook the reader. Ask, *What interests you in the lead? Do you want to know more about something? Did something just sound great?* Ask students, individually or in small groups, to choose a cover illustration of a book they haven't read (several can choose the same one) and write leads for what they think the book might be about.

Wrap-up

Invite students to share their leads, and hold a discussion about whether the leads do what they're intended to do. As with any peer-critique situation, students *must* speak respectfully about their peers' work. One way to ensure this is to require that students share one thing they like about the work before mentioning one thing they don't like.

Extension Activities

What Makes a Lead Tick?

Divide students into small groups, each of which gets a selection of picture books with strong lead sentences, and have students record the lead's *function. Does the lead describe the setting or characters? Does it move the reader right into the action? Is it a dialogue between main characters that introduces them both?* Challenge students to create categories for strong leads based on this research.

Dubbing in Leads

Remind the class of a well-known children's book, reviewing the story quickly with them. Then, in pairs, have students write possible leads for the book. Invite them to share the results, discuss their merits, and then read the original lead. Ask which leads students like best and why.

Literature Connection

Below are several books that feature provocative, question-producing leads:

Beezus and Ramona
by Beverly Cleary, 1955, An Avon Camelot Book, NY

> Beatrice Quimby's biggest problem was her little sister Ramona.

Charlotte's Web
by E. B. White, 1952, HarperCollins Publishers, NY

> "Where's Papa going with that axe?" said Fern to her mother as they were setting the table for breakfast.

Night of the Gargoyles
by Eve Bunting, 1995, The Trumpet Club, NY

> The gargoyles squat high on corners staring into space, their empty eyes unblinking til night comes.

George Shrinks
by William Joyce, 1985, Scholastic Inc., NY

> One day, while his mother and father were out, George dreamt he was small, and when he woke up he found it was true.

Shortcut
by Donald Crews, 1992, The Trumpet Club, NY (This lead also foreshadows the events of the story.)

> We looked…
> We listened…
> We decided to take the shortcut home.
> We should have taken the road.

Small Groups of Leads

WRITING CONNECTION

Challenge students to write three or four very different leads for either a piece of writing already under construction or a brand new one. Have students share and peer-review their leads in small groups, discussing which leads they prefer and why. Explain that in addition to being scrupulously careful of each other's feelings, discussion should focus on how leads function, what they reveal to readers, and what questions they bring up. They can certainly ask peer-authors what they were going for in their leads and which one they themselves prefer and why.

Writers' Wall

WRITERS' WALL

Exhibit great leads from published literature and from student writing. You might divide the Wall into kinds of leads.

Endings

Student Objective

To understand the function of the ending as providing a satisfying (or sometimes off-balancing) conclusion.

Background

Endings, of course, often tie together the bits and pieces of stories. But they can also be ambiguous or disturbing, requiring readers to interpret behavior or confront uncomfortable situations. However they affect us, they are crucial to the impact of the writing. As Ralph Fletcher writes in *What a Writer Needs*, "It is the ending, after all, that will resonate in the ear of the reader when the piece of writing has been finished. If the ending fails, the work fails in its entirety" (Fletcher, 92). Thus, student writers need to spend time crafting and revising endings just as they do beginnings.

Lesson

All's Well That End's Well or Sometimes Leaves You Hanging

Choose a great picture book and read it aloud, stopping before the ending. Then create a story web with your students, displaying the characters and their relationships. Have students, in small groups and with the story diagrammed in front of them, write their own endings. Explain in advance that, since endings echo in our imaginations, they are very important–they greatly affect our impression of the writing as a whole. (You might want to choose a book that ends ambiguously, since students tend to wrap things up happily or neatly.)

Wrap-up

Invite students to share their endings and discuss the choices they made, including not only plot decisions, but the manners in which they ended the story (abruptly, lingering over a character, in fantastic departures from the expected, and so on). Ask, for instance, *How does that ending make you feel about the characters? about the event? Is it a satisfying ending? Why or why not? Is it in keeping with the rest of the book? Do you agree that endings determine how you feel, what you think about the whole book?* Finally, share the author's original ending and discuss its merits.

Extension Activities

Conclusions About Endings

Divide students into small groups, each of which gets a selection of picture books with a variety of endings. Have students discuss the success of the endings: are they satisfying (either because they tie things together or leave them compellingly uncertain), or do they fall short? Groups summarize one of the books and analyze the ending, however they feel about it, and then share their conclusions with the class. Alternately, give each group a chapter book and have students look at how the end of each chapter hooks readers, compelling them to start the next chapter. Have students also summarize, analyze, and share the results of their research.

Literature Connection

Here are just a few books that feature a variety of kinds of endings:

Something from Nothing
by Phoebe Gilman, 1992, Scholastic Inc., NY

The Great Kapok Tree
by Lynne Cherry, 1990, Harcourt Brace Jovanovich, NY

Sam and the Tigers
by Julius Lester, 1996, Dial Books for Young Readers, NY

Cliff-Hangers

Challenge students to write cliff-hangers on long pieces of paper and then dangle them on clothes hangers somewhere in the classroom. Then have different students finish the stories. Host a student reading, and discuss whether the second authors finished the cliff-hangers as the first authors would have or took them in surprising directions. (This activity comes from *If You're Trying to Teach Kids How to Write, You've Gotta Have This Book!* by Marjorie Frank, 1979, Incentive Publications, Nashville.)

Bed-to-Bed, Beginning to End

Invite students to write "bed-to-bed," or circle, stories, which end where they begin. These are satisfying for young writers, who enjoy tying things up neatly, and so are great tools for practicing craft.

Below is a short list of bed-to-bed stories:

Millions of Cats
by Wanda Gag, 1928, Coward, McCann & Geoghegan, NY

The Ghost-Eyed Tree
by Bill Martin Jr. & John Archambault, 1985, Henry Holt & Co., NY

Where the Wild Things Are
by Maurice Sendak, 1963, HarperCollins Publishers, NY

Students can use the graphic organizer on page 85 to help them plan a circle story.

Writers' Wall

Exhibit great endings from published literature and from student writing. You might divide the Wall into kinds of endings, from the "neat" to the utterly ambiguous.

Circle Story

Plan your circle story on this page. Write your main character's name in the circle, and begin the story at your character's home. Then tell about the adventures your character will have, and be sure to end the story at home.

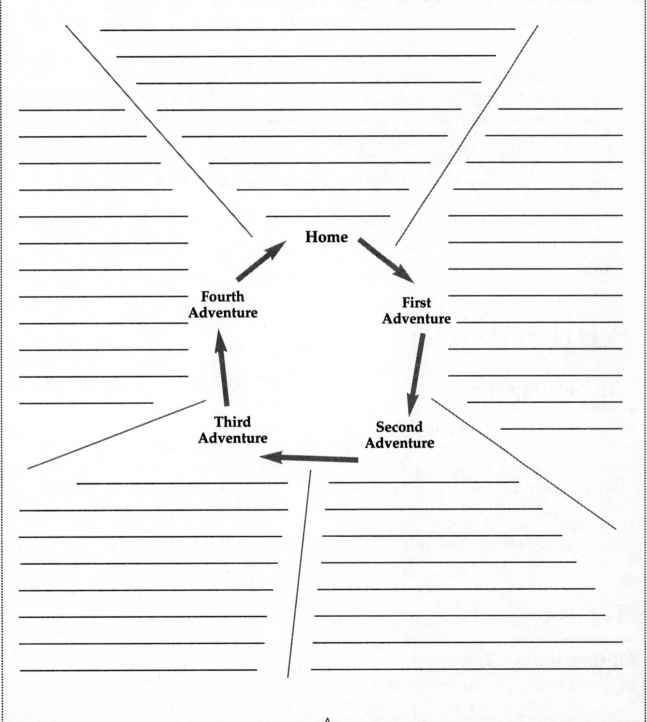

AUTHOR'S CRAFT

So far the focus has been on the mechanics of writing, though the beauty and power of language have come up, as they must, in the course of other topics. This section focuses on rhetorical devices and figurative language that are certainly essential—and often the most direct—ways to convey meaning, but that also charm, lull, coax, anger, mollify, and otherwise emotionally engage the reader.

Alliteration

Student Objective

To understand and enjoy alliteration.

Background

Alliteration is the repetition of beginning sounds of words, as in *Alex the animated aardvark always ate a lot.*

Lesson

Alliteration A—Z

Explain alliteration, and then invite volunteers to demonstrate it by reading the following poem aloud.

> Betty Botter bought some butter,
> "But," she said, "the butter's bitter.
> If I put it in my batter,
> It will make my batter bitter.
> But a bit of better butter,
> That would make my batter better."
> So she bought a bit of butter
> Better than her bitter butter,
> And she put it in her batter,
> And the batter was not bitter.
> So 'twas better Betty Botter
> Bought a bit of better butter.
>   —Anonymous

Wrap-up

Tell the class that they're going to build an acrostic alphabet poem, explaining that acrostics have "spines" that spell words or mean something vertically, and the letters of the spine also serve in words that run horizontally. (It will all become clear when they see it.) Assign each student a letter of the alphabet, starting again and doubling if you have more students than letters, and challenge them to alliterate sentences according to their assigned letters. Take *q*, *x*, and *z* yourself or do them as a class. When students are done, list the alphabet in capitals down the chalkboard, have students read their sentences aloud, and record them to make the acrostic. (Dictionaries might make this activity more fun and fruitful.)

Extension Activities

Tease, Tap, and Twist Your Tongue

ORAL LANGUAGE

Ask students if they know any tongue twisters, and invite them to recite them. Point out that not only is a good tongue twister alliterative, but it also switches kinds of sounds rapidly, making it difficult to wrap a tongue around. Challenge students to write their own tongue twisters (for inspiration, they can read one of the books in the Literature Connection), and then post them on the Writers' Wall.

Literature Connection

LITERATURE CONNECTION

Below are two books of tongue twisters:

World's Toughest Tongue Twisters
by Joseph Rosenbloom, 1987, Sterling Publishing Co., Inc, NY

> Little licorice lollipops. Little licorice lollipops. Little licorice lollipops.

Tongue Twisters
by Charles Keller, 1989, Simon & Schuster Books for Young Readers, NY

> Eight apes ate eight apples.
>
> Lucy loosened Suzie's shoes and Suzie's shoes stayed loose while Suzie snoozed.

The next book is a narrative that features alliteration:

Princess Prunella and the Purple Peanut
by Margaret Atwood, 1995, Workman Publishing, NY

> Princess Prunella lived in a pink palace with her pinheaded parents, Princess Patty and Prince Peter, her three plump pussycats, Patience, Prue, and Pringle, and her puppy-dog, Pug.

Poetry, of course, frequently uses alliteration. Invite students to find examples in their favorite poetry books.

Teaming With Tangled, Troubled Tongues

WRITING CONNECTION

Have students write and publish illustrated books of alliterative tongue twisters. They might even want to showcase their books at a class book fair for younger students.

Students Invent Ingenious Stories

WRITING CONNECTION

Using *Princess Prunella and the Purple Peanut*, have students write their own alliterative narrations. They can illustrate and publish these as well.

Writers' Wall

WRITERS' WALL

Post a list of alliteratively named characters (Jack and Jill, Miss Muffet, Bugs Bunny, Simple Simon, and so on) as a reference. Later, exhibit student tongue twisters and other alliterative writings.

Onomatopoeia

Student Objective

To understand onomatopoeia and how to use it.

Background

Onomatopoeia is making or using words that sound like what they mean, like *buzz, hum,* and *slurp.* English abounds in onomatopoetic words, some of which we use in common speech, some of which appear as effects (*Boom! Splat*). Of course, other languages use onomatopoeia as well, and students who speak other languages might enjoy sharing the ones they know. Words for animals' sounds are commonly onomatopoetic—while we say *Arf arf* or *Woof woof* for dogs' barking, in France they say *Ouah ouah,* in Italy *Bu bu,* and in Germany *Haf haf.*

Lesson

Onomatopoeia Sounds Like What It Is

Explain onomatopoeia, presenting examples (you might want to read from *Crash! Bang! Boom!,* below), and then have students brainstorm onomatopoetic words in small groups.

Wrap-up

Challenge students to invent new, accurate onomatopoetic words for sounds, animal or otherwise. Let them share their results. You might even have them research onomatopoetic words in other languages; they could interview people and research in the library or on line.

Extension Activities

ORAL LANGUAGE

Writing Sounds

Divide students into groups and give each group a tape recorder. Let them record sounds in the class and outside or provide them with tapes of sounds. The job is to invent words and spellings for the sounds they hear. (If using tape recorders is not an option, students can jot down descriptions of live sounds, and then figure out representative words and spellings later.) Students list their words on posters. When every group is ready (perhaps over several sessions), students try to figure out the sounds that the words represent. If sounds are unfamiliar, or to check success, students can match the words against the taped sounds.

(This is a useful prewriting activity for "*Crash!* Unhand Me!," below.)

ORAL LANGUAGE

What's the Sound of That?

As a class, brainstorm circumstances and locations in which it would be appropriate to use onomatopoeia, such as *barnyard, traffic jam, Indy raceway, eating as a large party at a restaurant, listening to waves,* and so on. Assign circumstances or locations to groups of three or four students, who then discuss the sorts of sounds they would hear and compile onomatopoetic words to represent them. Students share their lists of sound words, and the other students try to guess the circumstance or location they match.

ORAL LANGUAGE

Now That Word Says What It Means

Challenge small groups of students to think of onomatopoetic words used in common speech and writing—words that sound like what they mean but aren't just effects. Groups share their results with the class. Post these words on the Writers' Wall. (Dictionaries would be helpful for this activity.)

Literature Connection

Many poems use onomatopoeia; encourage students to bring in their favorites and share them with the class. Another source for onomatopoeia is the comic section of the newpaper.

Below are books that feature onomatopoeia:

Crash! Bang! Boom!
By Peter Spiers, 1972, Doubleday & Company, Inc., NY

Barnyard Banter
by Denise Fleming, 1994, Henry Holt & Co., NY

> Cows in the pasture,
> moo,
> moo,
> moo
> Roosters in the barnyard,
> cock-a-doodle-doo

Night Noises
by Mem Fox, 1989, The Trumpet Club, NY

> CREAK, CRACK
> went Lily Laceby's knees
> SNICK, SNACK
> went the bolts on the door.

Going on a Bear Hunt
by Michael Rosen, 1989, Margaret K. McElderry Books, NY

> Oh-oh! A river! A deep, cold river. We can't go over it. We can't go under it. Oh, no! We've got to go through it!
> Splash Splash!
> Splash Splash!
> Splash Splosh!

Ding Dong Ding Dong
by Margie Palatini, 1999, Hyperion Books for Children, NY

> Ding Dong
> Ding Dong

Slam! Bam! "SCRAM, you big ape!"
"EEEE-OOOOOOOOOOOOW!"
Oh, wow. Being a door-to-door salesman for Ape-On Cosmetics was no easy job.

OnomatoPoetry

Invite students to write onomatopoetic haiku. Remind them that they should choose subjects that lend themselves to using sound words. More ambitious students might want to use only onomatopoetic words that are *not* just effects.

> Crinch, crunch, crash, squeal,
> Varoom, squeal, rev, rev, roar,
> Indy Race winner

Crash! Unhand Me!

Using the taped sounds from "Writing Sounds," invite students to create their own radio plays. Students write stories that use the taped sounds, in the order they occur, as play scripts, and then perform them for the class, complete with sound effects. Alternately, let students record their own sounds to suit stories. They might even record the entire story—script and sound effects—and then play the tape for the class as if everyone were listening to the radio.

Smashing Funnies

Invite students to write and draw comic strips that incorporate onomatopoetic words. They might want to write about the circumstances or locations from "What's the Sound of That?"

Writers' Wall

Post sound words and also the not-just-effect words compiled for "Now That Word Says What It Means." Here are a few sound words to start off with:

gulp	roar	clunk	psst	pitter-pat
shhh	clang	bang	sizzle	clickety-clack
drip	hiss	cackle	clatter	varoom

Personification

Student Objective

To understand what personification is and how to use it.

Background

Personification, in literary terms, is the assigning of human qualities to nonhuman things and ideas. Personifying is a natural human activity—we do it all the time, speaking about *Mother Nature, Father Time,* and death as *The Grim Reaper.* And authors frequently employ personification because it is an immediately vivid way to convey ideas.

Lesson

I'd Like You to Meet Personification

Explain personification—what it is and why authors use it—presenting examples on the chalkboard. Students will probably be familiar with personifications such as The Man in the Moon, Old Man Winter, and Jack Frost. Ask, *What do you see when you think of these personified ideas? What does* Old Man Winter *look like?* Show them other more subtle kinds of personification: *the sun smiled on the fields; happiness led her by the hand; the tires screeched.*

Wrap-up

Read *Mirandy and Brother Wind* aloud (see Literature Connection, below) and discuss the personifications. Ask students to record them and others they think of, then post the list on the Writers' Wall as a reference

Extension Activities

Blinking Flags and Sleeping Trains

ORAL LANGUAGE

As a class, brainstorm 50 or more verbs (*sleep, race, wake, stretch, blink, cry, whisper, smile, shriek, wail, run,* and so on). Then divide students into small groups and give them different lists of objects (*clock, stream, clouds, moon, sun, flag, train, trees, stars, rocket, car, chair,* and so on). The groups then put the verbs and objects together into phrases or sentences that, if possible, personify the things appropriately. Explain that they should ask themselves, *If this were a person, what could it do?* Of course, many of the pairings will be more fantastic than accurately descriptive, but they will definitely be exciting!

> The moon rises, smiling kindly, and begins her quiet trip from east to west.

> The sunlight inched across the floor, spilling light into the cracks in the planks.

> The chair groans, rocking back and forth.

A Personification Looks Like...

ORAL LANGUAGE

Encourage students to illustrate the personifications from "Blinking Flags and Sleeping Trains." They can take turns displaying pictures to the class, which tries to guess what the illustration personifies.

Literature Connection

Of course, poetry makes frequent use of personification. Encourage students to bring in their favorite poetry books and share examples of personification that they especially like.

Here are several books that feature personification:

Northern Lullaby
by Nancy White Carlstrom, 1992, The Trumpet Club, NY
Illustrated by Leo and Diane Dillon (the pictures are spectacular)

> Goodnight Papa Star
> Goodnight Mama Moon,
> Bending your silver arms
> > down through the darkness.

Barn Dance!
by Bill Martin Jr. and John Archambault, 1986, The Trumpet Club, NY

> Then the skinny kid heard it…heard it faint begin…
> A plink! plink! plink! on the wind's violin…

Mojave and Heartland
by Diane Siebert, 1989 and 1992, respectively, HarperTrophy, NY

> I am the Heartland,
> Great and wide.
> I sing of hope.
> I sing of pride.

Mirandy and Brother Wind
by Patricia C. McKissack, 1988, The Trumpet Club, NY

> Swish! Swish!

It was spring, and Brother Wind was back. He come high steppin' through Ridgetop, dressed in his finest and trailing that long, silvery wind cape behind him.
Swoosh! Swoosh! Swoosh!

I'm a Word Puzzle

Challenge students to try their hands at personification riddles. Students think of objects and then describe them in detail as if they were people. (If they like, they can write rhyming riddles, as below.) Have students publish their riddles as flap books or post them on the Writers' Wall.

> I have bony fingers that point at you.
> I wave hello, or is it goodbye?
> You can only see my bony fingers in the winter.
> Who am I?
> Answer: a tree

If My Favorite Shirt Could Talk…

Have students write stories or poems that make rich use of personification. Let them choose between personifying a fruit or vegetable, a sound (this almost requires them to use onomatopoeia, too), or an article of clothing.

Writers' Wall

Post the list of personifications developed for the lesson as a reference.

Imagery (and Metaphor and Simile)

Student Objective

To use figurative language to paint word pictures.

Background

Imagery is the use of precise words or figurative language to create pictures in the mind of the reader. Personification is one kind of imagistic writing. Two others, to be explored in this section, are *metaphor* and *simile*. Metaphor is describing one thing as another thing that is not like it, as in the sentence, *The sun buzzed angrily over our heads*. The sun is being described as a bee. Simile is describing one thing by *comparing* it to another thing that is not like it, as in *The sun buzzed over our heads like an angry bee*. In the simile, the sun is still being thought of as a bee, but the description uses *like*, making explicit the fact that it is a comparison. (Similes require "comparing words" like *as* and *like*.)

The fabulous point of metaphors and similes is that by describing something in terms of a very different something else, we bring the thing we're describing to vivid life, revealing attributes and behaviors and perceptions we might otherwise never have noticed (maybe you once felt the sun was taking the whole thing a little too personally). In fact, that's the fabulous point about imagery in general.

Lesson

Word Paint

Explain that imagery is precise language that paints vivid pictures in readers' minds. Then invite volunteers to read aloud "What Is Gray?" from *Hailstones and Halibut Bones* (see the Literature Connection). Tell students to try to see the things the poem describes. Then, after two or three readings, ask, *Which images do you remember? Describe in your own words what you saw as a picture of one of the images.* Encourage students to elaborate on the poem's images by detailing their own mental pictures. Say, for instance, *When I think of the "falling-apart house," I see a tall Victorian house, set way back from the sidewalk and behind an iron fence at the end of an overgrown yard. What do you see? How does the image make you feel? What's the mood of the poem? And how does the poem achieve its mood?* Lead students to speak about the kinds and sounds of words in the poem. Ask finally, *Do you think the poem answers the question,* What is gray?, *successfully?*

> Gray is the color of an elephant
> And a mouse
> And a falling-apart house.
> It's fog and smog,
> Fine print and lint,
> It's a hush and
> The bubbling of oatmeal mush.
> Tiredness and oysters
> Both are gray,
> Smoke swirls
> And grandmother curls...

Wrap-up

Introduce *metaphor* and *simile*, using examples from the Background, above, or somewhere else (other than the poem). *Then ask, Are there any metaphors in "What Is Gray?"* Lead students to articulate that the description of gray in line four is a metaphor: it says gray is *fog* and *smog*. *Hailstones and Halibut Bones* is long on metaphor and short on simile, but you'll find many vivid similes in *Birdwatch*, also in the Literature

Connection. The woodpecker's "…swift/ ratatatatat," for example, is described "as casual as a jackhammer/ on a city street,/ as fine as a needle/ in a record groove,/ as cleansing as a dentist's probe/ in a mouthful of cavities…" Compile a short set of clear examples (three or four sentences) of imagery, metaphor, and simile for the Writers' Wall as a reference.

Extension Activities

The Amazing Technicolor Writing Assignment

Project swirling colors using an overhead and have students describe the images they see. (This activity comes from the poet Lee Bennett Hopkins.) Fill a glass pie-plate with water and set it on the overhead projector platform. Swirl the water and begin adding drops of food coloring to it. Students invent and write word pictures individually or in groups. Share the results and post them on the Writers' Wall.

Synaesthesia Signpost

Using *Hailstones and Halibut Bones* as a model, students pick colors (maybe out of the stock of crayons or from paint samples) and think up ways to see, smell, taste, and feel them. Individually or in groups, students record their ideas on large paper and post them on the Writers' Wall.

Finishing Like Writers

Write up simile beginnings on strips of paper and distribute them to small groups. Groups then complete the similes, writing the endings on separate strips. Groups then exchange strips, both the beginnings and the endings, and try to put each other's similes together. Share results and post favorite examples on the Writers' Wall. Simile beginnings might include:

The road was as winding as…
The clouds looked like…
The stream bubbled like…
The basketball player was as tall as…
The lightning looked like…
He was hungrier than …

What's It Like?

Divide students into three or four teams. Students work together to think up similes or metaphors (depending on which version of the game they're playing) that illustrate adjectives the game master (the teacher, usually) announces. Team members take turns presenting the team's answer. If the adjective were tall, for example, the spokesperson for one team might say, *The baby is as tall as a wolfhound.* The next team's spokesperson might say, *The tree is as tall as a giant*, and so on. Teams start with ten points, losing a point for every incorrect answer, such as making a sentence without a simile: *The giant is tall.* If they were playing the metaphor game, a correct answer might be, *The baby is a giraffe.* (Note: Metaphor is trickier for students to figure out, so while playing the game will be useful practice for them, it might be best to run through the simile version several times first.)

Literature Connection

Here are just a few of the many authors who paint vivid word pictures:

Hailstones and Halibut Bones
by Mary O'Neill, 1961, Doubleday & Company, Inc., NY

Birdwatch
by Jane Yolen, 1990, Fulcrum Press, NY

When I Was Young in the Mountains
by Cynthia Rylant, 1982, Puffin Unicorn Books, NY

On our way home, we stopped at Mr. Crawford's for a mound of white butter. Mr. Crawford and Mrs. Crawford looked alike and always smelled of sweet milk.

Frederick
by Leo Leonni, 1967, The Trumpet Club, NY
(Frederick is a poet mouse gathering images for his community.)

> "Frederick, why don't you work?" they asked.
> "I *do* work," said Frederick.
> "I gather sun rays for the cold dark winter days."

The next books feature vivid similes:

Owl Moon
by Jane Yolen, 1987, Scholastic Inc., NY

Quick as a Cricket
by Audrey Woods, 1982, Child's Play (International) Ltd.

> I'm as sad as a basset,
> I'm as happy as a lark,
> I'm as nice as a bunny,
> I'm as mean as a shark.

Seven Blind Mice
by Ed Young, 1992, Scholastic Inc., NY

> "Ah," said White Mouse. "Now I see.
> The something is
> > as sturdy as a pillar,
> > supple as a snake,
> > wide as a cliff,..."

As: A Surfeit of Similes
by Norton Juster, 1989, William Morrow & Company, Inc., NY

> As poor as a church mouse
> As thin as a rail
> As smooth as a porpoise
> As rough as a gale...

Encourage students to find metaphors in their favorite books and share them with the class.

Mixing Your Palette

Using the ideas from "The Amazing Technicolor Writing Assignment" and "Synaesthesia Signpost," and with *Hailstones and Halibut Bones* as a model, students can write

their own color poems. Encourage them to use vivid metaphors and similes.

Mixing Signals

Using the ideas from "The Amazing Technicolor Writing Assignment" and "Synaesthesia Signpost" again, students can write triante poems about colors, which follow the form:

> 1-word title
> 2 words for odor
> 3 words for texture
> 4 words for sightings
> 5 words for sounds
>
> Gray
> Musty Earthy
> Soft Cool Damp
> Storm Wind Lightning Hail
> Crashing Thundering Booming Whirring Banging

Class Word Portraits

For a class project, put together a book modeled after *Quick as a Cricket*. Students contribute similes (or metaphors) that describe themselves; each page presents a different student.

> Jeffrey runs as fast as a mouse being chased by a cat.
> Yolanda eats up math like Godzilla.

Connecting Simile by Simile

Have students work individually or in small groups at writing simile chains. Individual simile chains begin and end with the same simile. Group chains pass from student to student, growing simile by simile as they go; after the first student, all others begin their similes with the last word of the preceding simile. Teacher Alison Didier developed this activity.

> 1) A sunset is like a whisper.
> 2) A whisper is like a hummingbird's feather.

3) A hummingbird's feather is like my mother's song…

Didier wrote the following chain:

>   a friend's smile
> is like a spring crocus;
>   a spring crocus
> is as happy as a new butterfly;
>   a new butterfly
> is like an idea you have in a dream;
>   an idea you have in a dream
> is like a call from grandma;
>   getting a call from grandma
> is as sweet as a caramel shake;
>   a caramel shake
> is as welcome as a friend's smile.

Landscape in Words

Challenge students to put their knowledge of imagery to the test by painting a word landscape that conveys any place they choose (backyard, summer camp, the ocean, the mall, a junkyard) in vivid, evocative detail. Encourage students to use all the types of imagery in their arsenal. Don't worry if the results are deep, deep purple: this exercise is meant to let them stretch their wings. And revising overwrought descriptions at a later date would be an excellent exercise, too.

Writers' Wall

Post examples of imagery, metaphor, and simile compiled for the lesson as a reference. Later, exhibit student poems, simile chains, and any other writings students are proud of.

Small Words

Student Objective

To recognize when small words fit the bill.

Background

As students learn "sophisticated" long words, they naturally want to use them, and will often do so even when clarity and rhythm call for small ones. While students should of course be encouraged to pick up and try out words they discover, they also should be shown that good writing is made of long and short words balanced around a purpose. While a long word may raise mental eyebrows, it's the contrapuntal short word that will, as Richard Lederer says in *The Miracle of Language*, "make a straight point between two minds" (Lederer, 34).

Lesson

Short and Sweet

Discuss the need for knowing when to use short words in writing. Then pair students and have them write directions for very simple tasks (making a peanut butter and jelly sandwich, walking a dog, sweeping a floor, and so on) using the fanciest, longest, most sophisticated language they can.

Wrap-up

When all the directions are written, let students share the results, which should be so ludicrous that the virtue of short words will be clear to all. But do point out also that sometimes a big word is more precise than one or two small ones, and in that case the bigger word may well be the better choice. For instance, rather than writing *very angry, very tired, or right on time,* it might be better in a given piece of writing to use *furious, exhausted,* and *punctual.*

Extension Activities

Market Research
ORAL LANGUAGE

Arrange students in small groups and hand out magazines with advertisements and collections of quotations. Groups then investigate the use of small words. They can even draw graphs that show numbers of small words per sentence in ads or quotations. Share results.

A Single Azure Piscine Companion...
ORAL LANGUAGE

Invite students to rewrite their favorite Dr. Seuss books, using long words wherever they can. When they're finished, hold readings of both the original text and the student revisions. The results should be amusing.

Short-Short-Word Short Stories
WRITING CONNECTION

Challenge students to write stories or expository compositions using only one-syllable words. Richard Lederer asks students to do the same and quotes one of his ninth graders, Celia Wren:

> For a long time we cruised by the coast and at last came to a wide bay past the curve of a hill, at the end of which lay a small town. Our long boat ride at an end, we all stretched and stood up to watch as the boat nosed its way in (*The Miracle of Language*, 36).

Writers' Wall
WRITERS' WALL

Exhibit strong one-syllable-word sentences (such as the student story quoted in "Short-Short-Word Short Stories") as references. Later, post short-word student work that they're especially proud of.